Testimonies from the Sweet Inspiration Callers:

I believe God, I trust God, and I thank you for all your prayers, I love you Mother Hines!

Theresa Spikes

Mother, You said, "within 72 hours God is going to work on behalf of those on **Sweet Inspirations**." Well my husband went from being Sgt.. Murray to Chief Murray today. He got a substantial raise and is Chief of Police for the Community College. I expect to give you many more reports. Blessings are coming on the heels of each other to me and everyone connected to me. Thank you for **Sweet Inspirations**. Your daily words have strengthened me thru the hardest times of my life.

Camona Murray
Charlottesville, VA

I am so thankful that God has been using Mother Hines to speak to me on life. I always look forward to hearing a word from you. You are truly anointed. Glory to God! I pray that God continues to anoint you to bless others and pour supernatural favor upon your life. God Bless You!

A Sweet Inspiration's Caller

Mother Hines, you have been speaking to us about faith, miracles, and the blessings upon blessings on the heels of another and it is happening just like THAT! I released my New Years SEED, and sowed in several offerings. I prayed over it before releasing and directed it to where I wanted it to go. I auditioned for a supporting role in a new play and was chosen for the LEAD! Then on my day job, I am up for a higher position and increase on a new contract that far exceeds my current salary! God did more than I expected.

Reisha Simpson
Delaware

My mother asked me to come to a church revival where I heard you. I have been battling an abusive relationship for 3 years. Not even 3 hours after I left the church, my abusive man got pulled over in my car. This arrest will give me the time I need to grow. The police officer even let me come get my car. I'm not saved. I know God, but I'm not ready yet. I never believed He still heard my cries; but now I know He does.

Melanie W

Mother, I no longer have thoughts of divorce! **Hallelujah Thank You Jesus!** I received what you told me to do...love my husband!! I know GOD is working on me, my husband, and my children. Also, my daughter in St. Louis has a new job making more money!! **Glory be to GOD! Hallelujah**!! I believe GOD!! I thank GOD for you taking the time out to talk to me and give me Godly advice. This is just the beginning of my praise report. Before I was having a battle in my mind about divorcing my husband...**but GOD!!!** I love my husband!! Now I expect complete restoration of my marriage **Glory be to GOD! Amen!**

Sweet Inspirations Caller

Praise Report! I sowed into your ministry and attached a request of the Lord on behalf of my son. He is a 26 years old, college educated, hardworking young man. He has a job, but was looking for a better paying job that would help him build his career. In this last year he had filled out somewhere close to 1,000 job applications and was only contacted by approximately 2% of them. It had been wearing him down and I asked God to intervene with my gift. The week I gave the gift, he had an interview that ended up offering him the job – with better pay, tuition assistance (he wants to pursue his MBA) and an opportunity to begin the path of a project manager. Our God is faithful and just. Blessed be His name forever and ever! There is a greater call on my son's life and I am believing for the promise over his life to come into fruition. May God continue to bless you Mother.

Pebbles Brown-Leonard

The Morning Cup

A SWEET INSPIRATIONS COLLECTION ~ VOL II

The Morning Cup

A Sweet Inspirations Collection ~ Vol II

Mother Judy Hines

Copyright © 2019 Mother Judy Hines

All rights reserved. No part of this publication may be reproduced, distributed, or transmitted in any form or by any means, including photocopying, recording, or other electronic or mechanical methods, without the prior written permission of the publisher, except in the case of brief quotations embodied in critical reviews and certain other noncommercial uses permitted by copyright law. For permission requests, write to the publisher, addressed "Attention: Permissions Coordinator," at the address below.

ISBN: 978-1-7322879-5-2 (Paperback)

Any references to historical events, real people, or real places are used fictitiously. Names, characters, and places are products of the author's imagination.

Front cover images: NordWood Themes and lumix2004
Book and cover design by Tracy Fagan

First printing edition 2019

Kingdom Publishing
PO Box 653
Parker, CO 80134

www.kingdom-publishing.com
For purchasing this book in bulk, please contact the publisher directly.

Contact Mother Judy Hines by e-mail at motherjudyhines@gmail.com or through her website www.OvercomerIntlNet.org.

Join the Call!

712-775-8919
Access Code 383023
Mon.-Fri. 7:00a-7:15a (ET)

*This is the call God has designed to get you up and moving, and to bring you **one step closer** to your **predestined position in Him**.*

*We are committed to living the best life in Him and therefore **becoming spiritually, financially and physically fit**.*

Table of Contents

Welcome!........................... 13

Introduction 15

The Kingdom Answer 19

Give Us This Day Our Daily Bread 39

Sitting 63

Give Thanks to the Lord Always! 79

Watch and Pray (Agrupneo).............. 91

Gratitude is the Way to Success 113

Every Space Must Be Filled With Praise.... 133

A Tribute 155

There is Power and Purpose in Your Praise .. 175

About Psalm 92 193

Revive!............................ 211

Just Begin... 225

About the Author.................... 239

Welcome!

The Morning Cup: A Sweet Inspirations Collection Volume II *is a continuation of our daily celebrations & inspirations that have uplifted readers worldwide for over ten years. Yes! This year we are celebrating ten years of Sweet Inspirations with Mother Judy Hines!*

I thank each and every one of you for your continued support! It is with your support that we have amassed a global following of over 10 million! As we head into our tenth year, we are in expectation of God to continue to move mightily as we reach to new heights, dimensions, and horizons!

As you begin to read Volume II, I pray that you will truly allow the Father to communicate with you. I pray you will learn what it truly means to have that personal relationship with the Father. Master your time with the Father and as you give yourself away, the Father will take care of your life. Be encouraged! You are blessed beyond measure. You are strengthened by His peace and refueled by His joy. No Matter what it looks like, we WIN in HIM!

Sweet Inspirations to you and each of you much, much Love,

Mother Judy Hines

Introduction

Good morning, everyone. Thank you so much for calling in every Monday through Friday 7:00 am to 7:15 am, Eastern Standard Time. This is the call God has designed to get you up and moving, and to bring you one step closer to your predestined position in Him. We are committed to living the best life in Him and therefore becoming spiritually, financially and physically fit.

We are continuing the journey and pressing toward the mark! I am elated to present this body of work to you. **The Morning Cup: A Sweet Inspirations Collection Volume II** is intended to inspire, empower, uplift, and edify. It is purposed to remind you, who you are & whose you are! Often times throughout our lives we face challenges and difficulties. Whatever the trouble you are facing, the list may seem endless, but God has not changed His mind concerning you.

SWEET INSPIRATIONS

INTRODUCTION

God says you are quality in the kingdom, and you are valuable to the kingdom. He has equipped you to do that very thing that no one else has yet to do! You are called to greater works! In this book I know the Father is truly going reveal to you a strategic plan for excelling your spiritual gifts with power and authority.

I pray the words along these pages would renew your mind and refresh your spirit. I decree that today is the beginning of your best days and that you will begin living your best life! Old things have passed away, all things have become new! You have the power to change your atmosphere and circumstance. Start anew today and let go the things of the past. Seek the face of God and stay in His presence, allow His transformative power to do a work in you! Hallelujah.

God is sending forth his people, an unnamed army that is going forth in powerful demonstrations of signs, wonders, miracles, and healings. It is time for us to soar like Eagles. ***The Morning Cup, A Sweet Inspirations Collection Volume II*** is your Clarion Call! Take a seat, grab your coffee and get ready to be welcomed into your next position in God!

Much Love,
Mother Judy Hines

SWEET INSPIRATIONS

CHAPTER 1
The Kingdom Answer

When we pray, we pray, "Thy Kingdom come." We have entered into God's Kingdom when we accept Christ as our Savior or when we become born again. We enter into the Kingdom of God in this dimension as it embodies the way God does things. In this dimension, we discover how God acts and performs His wondrous deeds. We are called into the earthly realm by praying and we are called into the Kingdom realm by praying. I said that twice, earth and Kingdom, because I want you to understand the vitally important role of prayer in our lives.

We are called, in this earthly realm, to pray and ask God to send us a Kingdom answer. There is a Kingdom answer to every need you have. Jesus said that it should be on earth the way it is in Heaven. What you are really asking is for the Father to not only send the Kingdom of God to earth, but you want and need the revelation in your heart, as well.

We can alter and make adjustments in our lives that can coordinate to the scriptures and the will of God. So, we want His revelation to make the necessary adjustments to become like Him. We want to live in this dimension so Jesus taught us to say, "Thy will be done on earth as it is in Heaven." The problem with that is most of us have never thought about or imagined what Heaven is really like.

> Think about a dimension where all the *power of God* is represented in *ultimate perfection.*

But, this morning, let's daydream a little bit. Let's think about being free—free of illness, free of afflictions, free of lack, free of poverty. Let's think about being free of any and all oppression. Just think about it. Think about a dimension where all the power of God is represented in ultimate perfection. Think about it; because when we think about something, it changes our way of viewing it. The Lord works within you to change your mindset, your reference point. We think about being free of depression, oppression, and suppression—free of all negativity. Imagine if you are free of all of that, what type of positive energy you will have? Imagine what types of creativity the Lord can unleash in you? Listen, you are going to have some real tangible inner power, maybe like you have never really felt before

THE KINGDOM ANSWER

because **there will be nothing then that can stand against you!**

You will have no rivals, no plots against you, no plans that undermine you, and no schemes to bamboozle you. The backstabbing will cease.

You will not have ANY of those opponents out on the perimeter of your life affecting you, a Child of God. You will feel so free to live in the presence and the glory of God that it will truly feel like a brand new day! You will feel, maybe for the first time in quite a while, the freedom to make progress and assert yourself in your mission, your vision, and whatever it is God calls you to do now. There will be no stopping you. So, right now, God wants you to live like that. He needs you to live like you are in His Kingdom right now, where there is no stopping you.

> You will feel so *free to live* in the presence and the glory of God that it will truly *feel like a brand new day!*

SWEET INSPIRATIONS

REFLECT

Capture the emotions and feelings you are experiencing as you dream about Heaven.

....
....
....
....
....
....
....
....
....
....
....
....
....
....
....
....
....
....
....
....
....

THE KINGDOM ANSWER

You are unstoppable. You are unbeatable. That friends, is the "Kingdom Mind." Whatever is happening in the Kingdom, is happening here on earth. God never sees us in a "weakened condition" or in our "inadequacy," but rather, He sees us the way He intends for us to be—exactly as He made us; as He envisioned each of us "In the beginning..." He created us to overcome, win, and achieve.

Oh yes, you ARE going over that wall today!

You are going over that wall and racing through the troops today because you now have your real mindset—as God intends it. This is the real you, and you now can run with Kingdom on your mind.

> Now have your real mindset—
> as God intends it.
> *This is the real you!*

REFLECT

List characteristics of the real you.
What gifts have God given you to build the kingdom?

....
....
....
....

SWEET INSPIRATIONS

THE KINGDOM ANSWER

When you think about Heaven, you are also thinking about the strength of God. The strength of God causes you to be strong even in your weakness. His strength causes you to be stronger because His strength grows in you. That is what He did for Paul. God's grace was sufficient. His strength was sufficient. What you really have here is the supernatural, God, expressing Himself in the natural—our worldly existence. When we pray, "Thy Kingdom come, Thy will be done on earth as it is in Heaven," He is about to express Himself in the natural realm. God stretches out in the natural realm and He is about to do something in the realm of nature. So, when He comes to earth, let's remember, He does not come through the front door of our lives to sit in our recliner and put his feet up!

Oh no, He comes on behalf of you.

He comes to see His people and He comes to make sure we are who we say we are—the prosperous, the overcomers, the winners, yes, the champions! He comes to make manifest, to bring to fruition with the fullness of time in His Hands. The Lord demonstrates His power and glory every second of every day. This is His reason and purpose for being in the world.

> The *strength of God* causes you to be strong *even in your weakness.*

REFLECT

List an area(s) of weakness for you. How have you seen God's strength in your weakness?

....
....
....
....
....
....
....
....
....
....
....
....
....
....
....
....
....
....
....
....
....

THE KINGDOM ANSWER

So when we say, "Thy will be done on earth as it is in Heaven," we give Him access to come into this earthly realm. The supernatural, which is God Himself, comes into the natural realm. Remember, His Word is His will. I know you hear me say this all the time and we must continually and everlastingly study to show ourselves approved unto God.

When we study, as in II Timothy 2:15 ("...study to show ourselves approved unto God..."), our prayer life immediately takes on the power of His answers. Whatever is in Heaven has now come to earth. You are now praying His Word, His solutions, so you cannot help but get His answers. Your prayer life takes on the power of God's answers because you are praying His Word. You are praying the answer. You are praying His will; and friend, I want you to know that deep in your heart and soul.

> Our prayer life *immediately* takes on *the power of His answers.*

That is powerful right there. You will then see His Word come to life. You will see a full demonstration of His power. You will see His glory and how God hastens to perform His Word. That means He gets up very quickly. The Word is quick, sharp, and powerful because God Himself, when you speak His Word, **h-a-s-t-e-n-s** to perform His Word. He does it quickly.

> Don't pray your problem.
> *Pray His answer*
> —The Kingdom Answer.

So, when you want to see a quick return or a quick result, simply use His Word.

Don't pray your problem. Pray His answer—The Kingdom Answer.

His Word is full of Kingdom Answers, or rather, His Word is a Kingdom full of Answers! It's time for all of us to "Go Kingdom!" Go all the way Kingdom! Let us all get Kingdom-minded right this moment. We find, in the Word, scriptures that apply to our requests and we pray those scriptures as prayer. Instead of trying to figure out what to say, just open up the Book! **Open up your Bible and pray those scriptures as prayer.** God will hasten to perform His Word. He will come quickly. He will arise and He will come quickly and give you results. That is His promise. The Promise-keeper Himself, the One who gets up, the One who fulfills prophecy; the One Who Causes the Word Not to Come Back Void—He is coming, He hastens, He quickly performs His Word.

THE KINGDOM ANSWER

REFLECT

List out 2-3 "problems" in your life. Find scripture that speaks to those issues and write a prayer based on Kingdom Answers. Mark this page and come back and record how God has answered your prayer.

....
....
....
....
....
....
....
....
....
....
....
....
....
....
....
....
....
....
....
....

So, we need to become more effective in praying the Word and in doing so we find the Word alone is sufficient for manifestation. The Word alone is also sufficient for those things that we have not yet seen come into manifestation. Perhaps we need to find the scripture that deals with it and begin to pray that scripture.

I want you to remember one thing; there IS a Kingdom Answer for every single need you could possibly have now or that you could possibly ever have in the future. God is the One who gives us that through His Word. The name of God means Word. He is His Word. His Word is most powerful and does not come back void. His Word accomplishes the thing that it is sent out to do. It leaves your mouth in the form of a word, but it always comes back in manifestation.

> It leaves your mouth in the *form of a word,* but it always *comes back in manifestation.*

Manifestation is a person, a place, or a thing.
So, what is it, right now that you stand in need of?
What is the request? As we say, who has a prayer request?
You ought to know now that I am going somewhere. We need to pray the scripture, because that is the answer, the Kingdom answer.

THE KINGDOM ANSWER

I hope this breaks it down simply enough for you, to inspire you now to **study the Word like you never have before because this is the golden treasure.** In the Word is life and in the Word is light; in the Word is abundance and prosperity because that is Who the Word is and the Word is God and He is all of those things. The Lord God is our Kingdom and our Kingdom Answer. He gives us His Word and in His Word there is a Kingdom answer for every need.

REFLECT

What is manifesting in your life? Think on what words have been coming out of your mouth - journal the correlation. What changes do you commit to make?

....
....
....
....
....
....
....
....
....
....
....
....

SWEET INSPIRATIONS

THE KINGDOM ANSWER

As you study and pray, you expand the Kingdom of God and bring His Kingdom to life. You can increase His Kingdom into the life of others who really need it when you come into contact with them. You can bring someone else into a breakthrough. His Word brings light and dispels the darkness. We want everyone in this world to experience what we are experiencing. God brings people your way. You are going to be their lifeline. Sometimes, when we start on our journey with God, on our creative venture with God, on our mission with God, when we go out into the world and interact with others it might not seem like much at first glance.

But anything God gives you is phenomenal. What God gives us is bigger than big and biggest of all. Just you watch where God takes it. The person at the bus stop who is waiting for the bus with you might need it most in their lives when you ask them,

"Do you know what time this bus usually gets here?"

They might need that question from a child of God more than you can ever know. Your question might greatly increase their self-worth in that moment because you found that child of God to be someone

> But *anything* God gives you is *phenomenal*.

who could help you. So, be encouraged throughout this day. Keep hanging in there! Prayer is the foundational piece that causes every ministry to flourish, every ministry to be effective and to reach its fullest potential, and that is what we need in this world. If this country or any other country needs anything, it is those who will pray, those who will stand in the gap, and those who will get up on the wall and who will call out to God on their behalf. What you are doing right now is very important and vital to the mission of God.

In Chapter Two, "Give Us This Day Our Daily Bread," we will discover what to look for when we find ourselves, and we all do from time to time, in a sort of "wilderness."

Have a wonderful, Jesus-filled day, blessings on each and every one of you, and be safe out there because I know you just got up and moving. I will talk to you in the morning. God bless.

THE KINGDOM ANSWER

REFLECT

Name something phenomenal the Lord has recently given you. Put a praise on it!

....
....
....
....
....
....
....
....
....
....
....
....
....
....
....
....
....
....
....
....

SWEET INSPIRATIONS
NOTES

THE KINGDOM ANSWER

SWEET INSPIRATIONS

CHAPTER 2
Give Us This Day Our Daily Bread

Something dazzling and new has appeared on our horizon. I feel it and sense it. I can tell it and I know God is up to something where His people are concerned. There is a brand new freshness here, like the bracing wind out on the ocean. We now must get over the "usual" and the "mundane" because this comes to us from the cutting edge. This is not coming from the routine point of reference or from the angle

> God challenges us all to see Him in *forever changing ways!*

we usually see things from. God challenges us all to see Him in forever changing ways! He challenges us to receive

Him in a various ways because we cannot ever say we know definitively about God. His flower unfolds eternally.

The Lord is winding up to throw a monkey wrench in here. He is about to pitch a most magnificent curve ball. You know, in baseball, even the best hitters, the ones who win the batting titles or are counted on for driving in the runs when all the chips are down, even they have a lot of trouble with the curve ball. Sometimes, you will see a player watch the baseball zing into a catcher's mitt and they will just kind of shake their heads a little bit. They must be saying to themselves something like, "Wow—can you believe that? It started out way over there, on the outside, but it ended up right over the plate just as it got to me. Or, it started out on a line directly over the plate and I just knew I had to swing at this one, but by the time it got to me it was wa-a-y out over there!"

That was a curve ball.

Well, the Lord knows we have trouble with the curve and that is precisely why he is pitching us one. He is about to let us know another dimension of Him that we have never ever tapped into before. I am excited and ready to receive the King today.

GIVE US THIS DAY OUR DAILY BREAD

REFLECT

The best way baseball players prepare for hitting curve balls is to study the pitcher. Take some time to study who God is. Journal below about some of your past experiences with Him.

SWEET INSPIRATIONS

*I*n Chapter One, we talked about "Thy kingdom come, Thy will be done in the earth as it is in Heaven." We want to continue now and take a look at the next part of the Lord's Prayer saying, "Give us this day our daily bread." Here, we are addressing Jehovah Jireh. We are addressing God, the Provider and asking Him to provide us our daily bread. In other words, yesterday has now passed and we have this day, today, to "...rejoice and be glad in it."

It is He who supplies all our needs according to His riches in glory by Christ Jesus. We need to understand today, right now, that He is not going to, but He is supplying our every need. This is not something He will do. He is doing it right now. In Chapter One, we learned about The Kingdom Answer to every single need we have and it is found in the scriptures. Philippians says,

> He **is** supplying our *every need.*

> *...nothing escapes His sights and heart for your needs can cover much ground but nothing, nothing is going to escape God's sight and nothing is going to escape His heart where your needs are concerned.*

In other words, He's got this. He is the One in control and he is the One we can give everything over to. We can relax and simply praise. In this way, we let the enemy know

GIVE US THIS DAY OUR DAILY BREAD

we are not worried about what he is doing. Oh, no. We really do not have time for that any more!

You are focused, your mind is set and your heart is fixed. You know God has this. That is the reason we praise. We can praise in the midst of adversity because we know God controls things and has only what is in our best interest on His mind and in His heart.

We already know the outcome.

We win.

We must firmly establish in our hearts and minds and agree with God that we are the winners. Even though our needs cover a lot of ground, nothing escapes Him. You don't have to worry about whether He sees, whether He knows or whether He's there. He IS there in that moment with you. He is the One giving you that strength you feel—the strength to go through whatever is there before you in the appearance of an obstacle. He is the One taking that power out of the fire and out of that collision. It could have been much, much worse but He is in this with you.

> *Agree with God that we are the winners.*

SWEET INSPIRATIONS

REFLECT

Say this aloud and write it down: **"No matter what I am going through, God is in it with me. He is going to take care of me and I am coming out on top. I am coming out all right."**

....
....
....
....
....

Journal about your past experience with
God when He provided.

....
....
....
....
....
....
....
....
....
....
....
....

GIVE US THIS DAY OUR DAILY BREAD

Listen to this and keep it in your heart: Jehovah Jireh literally means "God who sees ahead." We say it means "Our Provider," but it literally means "God who sees ahead."

"God knew my daily needs ahead of all time, since before time was, and He made advanced provisions for all of my needs."

> Jehovah Jireh literally means *"God who sees ahead."*

That's wonderful news right there! He knew your needs ahead of time. God, who sees ahead; knows what is coming **way down the road** and **He's already got it under control.** You don't have to sweat it, you don't have to faint and you don't have to be weary. God has it all under control.

I want you to see that when He said, "Let us make man," He knew of everything you could possibly need on your journey and made sure He had provided. So, right now I don't know if you can put it to a song or a tune, but you need to be humming, "He has already provided." No matter what it looks like or feels like, He has already provided.

Yes, that thing that caught you off guard and that thing that you had not anticipated, that curve ball, He already knew it was coming. He has taken care of it already.

Relax.

GIVE US THIS DAY OUR DAILY BREAD

Remember our exercise at the beginning of the chapter—simply begin to praise Him!

He foreknew everything, so He made advanced provisions for your needs. So, in your prayers, you travel a course bringing you to intersect His supply for you!

That wonderful statement bears repeating and this time let's personalize it.

In my prayers, I travel a course bringing me to intersect His supply for me!

REFLECT

Say this aloud and write it down: **"God knew my daily needs ahead of all time, since before time was, and He made advanced provisions for all of my needs."**

....
....
....
....
....

Write out a praise. Thank God in advance. Look in the book of Psalms to see examples of how others have written out praises to God.

....
....
....

SWEET INSPIRATIONS

GIVE US THIS DAY OUR DAILY BREAD

God orders your footsteps and lines up your location with His supply. He leads you right to what you need. He leads you right to your provision. He leads you right to the next dimension. He is going to lead you right to the next open door. He is going to your next check, your next promotion, your next elevation. Whatever your "next" is, God is leading you to it because He is causing you to intersect with your supply. It is the supply He set up for you before the foundation of the world! Now, isn't that something?

You thought you just got the problem a few days ago, but He foreknew, He looked ahead of time and saw what you were going to run into and He's already set up provisions. He has already set into motion the best solution. He has already provided the answer and that is the reason we began the chapter with nothing but praise! We need you to breathe in and breathe out because God will not let you down. Yes, He remains your Supplier and your Provider.

But He is your Redeemer, your Savior, your High Tower.

> We need you to *breathe in and breathe out* because God will not *let you down.*

He is your everything that you can possibly need Him to be and for that we must give Him even yet more praise! "The One Who Keeps Israel" does not sleep or slumber. He will not allow your feet to stumble. He will not allow you to fall or faint and He will not, He cannot, allow reproach to get the best of you. He will not allow the enemy to just walk up on you any kind of a way. You are coming out victorious and on victory ground and you may as well keep on praising because today your name is victory.

God tells us this day He brings that enemy into your hands and you are going to see a difference in your situation and your circumstances. You will see a difference in your children and spouse. You will begin to see a major difference because the Hand of God touches them today. He wants you to know that "touch" is a part of your daily bread.

Someone reading these words right this second needs God to touch in all of these areas because that someone has extreme and excruciating circumstances, but God is touching you today. God brings the supernatural touch you need right now.

I do not know who in particular that was for, but let us thank God that He touches us today.

GIVE US THIS DAY OUR DAILY BREAD

REFLECT

What do you need God to touch today? Decree and declare the change you want to see in your circumstances. Put a praise on it!

Find or make up a short song lyric that you can repeat throughout the day to praise God.

So, we know you and your supply will intersect. As you walk through that place you think is the wilderness, you will find what you need and what God wants you to have. Think of the Israelites wandering through the desert, when Manna fell from Heaven, they were allowed to take only what the day would demand for their well-being. Sometimes, we try to jump ahead and gather for the future. We're trying to stay way ahead. But this particular verse we are focusing on reads: "Give us this day our daily bread." If the Israelites took too much Manna, it would spoil! So, we want our daily bread today and God says to us He's going to show up in our daily bread and you are going to know it is the hand of God.

You expect your daily bread the usual way except…God is now going to come a brand new way. You were expecting your daily bread through the same person. No. God has decided you need Him to come to you in a brand new way. He is coming in a different way and a different manner. So, you need to get on your P's and Q's so you will be ready.

Remember, the children of Israel could take only enough Manna for the day except for the weekend when they could take an extra portion to meet the need until the Sabbath passed. Isn't that amazing? This is what God used to build their faith and this is what God uses to build our faith from day to day. Our day to day operation is from faith to faith and from glory to glory. This is why we pray,

GIVE US THIS DAY OUR DAILY BREAD

"Give us this day our daily bread." We depend completely on God each day to give us our provisions and to give us what we need throughout the course of a day. I want you to know something you may not fully believe: It is already done! Before you even got here, before you entered the field of time, before you entered into this earthly realm, it was already done for you! That is the reason we started to praise God at the beginning of this chapter. For you information,

> Before you even got here,
> before you entered the field of time,
> before you entered into this earthly realm,
> *it was already done for you!*

He's done, He's already peeked into your future. He's already looked into your future and He already knows the things you need. He is a good Father and He is going to give you the things you need—not only what you need but He gives us some things we want. He also gives you an overflow. He allows you to have a surplus and a bounty. You will not only have what you need but God is going to allow you, and give through you, a blessing to other people and other families.

SWEET INSPIRATIONS

REFLECT

What does "blessed to be a blessing" look like to you? How much do you need in order to be a blessing for others?

GIVE US THIS DAY OUR DAILY BREAD

God has positioned you into a wonderful place today. You are seated in heavenly places in Christ Jesus, but you are also seated in the dimension where you will be a blessing to others and to families. It wasn't only about your provisions. He made provisions for everyone reading or listening to these words. Every person's situation is different, but God has met the demand already! That is why we praise Him! We can truly sing this song. Praise is what I do. Praise is what we do! We give God thanks and we give Him glory because He looked ahead and saw our needs and He didn't judge us because of our flaws or our inadequacies. He looked ahead and even though we were a hot mess, He decided He would go to the cross and die for us. He decided He would bless us and He would still be our God and our Father.

> *God has met the demand already!*

This is the day God has made! He is going to make the difference in our lives and in the lives of the people around us! So, *Sweet Inspirations* readers and listeners, get ready for something new and different!

Yesterday, I had a photo session because our Dream Team said I needed new pictures. I hadn't had any real pictures taken in several years and it entailed quite a bit. I wanted to take some pictures with the phone camera like I normally do. But photo sessions are different. I had to get a stylist and a professional photographer. Now, I'm certain almost all of you know a stylist decides on and then receives the apparel, cosmetics, hairstyle, etc. I have to tell you, I did not like the items she, along with the assistance of my daughter, had chosen for me. However, after I saw the photographs I fell in love with what they had created. They had created a new me! I had to admit that the hand of God was influencing the entire project. If it had been left up to me, I still would have come out looking like yesterday instead of where I am today, who I am today, and where I am going. I needed the stylist, hairdresser, and photographer and I had to get a team approach to make all the difference. Believe me, it was really something. God assembled that team! They worked together in harmony, being guided by The One other team member.

The point I am making is now we have to do things differently, and even though we don't want to, it is most necessary because God is coming and approaching us in His brand new way. I want you to remember God is coming and approaching in newness, with excitement, and coming to change us into His very image. He causes us to become better and to act in different ways. We must not resist change. Change denotes growth. Without change there is no growth.

I do not know why I am saying this, but if you have a

GIVE US THIS DAY OUR DAILY BREAD

doily on your head, you might want to snatch it off because it is a new day, a brand new day in Zion. If you feel like you just can't wear anything but black and white, you might want to get someone to take you out and put some color on you. This is your assignment today. Go and do something today that changes something about you today.

> *Do something today that changes something about you today.*

Maybe you just wear dark "winter" colors in your wardrobe—purples, blues, blacks and browns. Maybe you want to go out in some "autumn" tones like yellow, orange, red, or tan and see how it changes your feeling. You are going to have to get accustomed to the new. Look at this; every time we go to church, we tell God we want something new and we are expecting a new day. Well, if we are expecting a new day, we are going to have to change some of the things that we are doing. We cannot keep doing the same thing and thinking we are going to get a different result. That makes no sense. I tried it for a long time until I realized that if I wanted something different I was going to have to do something differently. If I want something out of the ordinary, I am going to have to do something out of the ordinary.

SWEET INSPIRATIONS

REFLECT

What is at least one new thing you are committed to trying today? What is your biggest fear about trying it? Come back and journal what you experienced with the change.

....
....
....
....
....
....
....
....
....
....
....
....
....
....
....
....
....
....
....
....

GIVE US THIS DAY OUR DAILY BREAD

I don't know why I am still on this, but I'm teaching real hard and I am reaching for that one person reading these words who might feel a little timid to take a step of faith and do something out of the ordinary. Maybe that is the reason you have not accomplished your mission, your assignment, or your dream. It may not line up with what you see other people doing. Beware of comparing your actions to those of others. Just know that God has given it into your hands and He has already caused it to prosper. You are all ready and you are already there.

> All you need to do is *take a step*. Just begin and take a step.

All you need to do is take a step. Just begin and take a step. Each time you take a step, God will shed light on the next step and you will find yourself picking up momentum and picking up the pace and after a while it won't bother you about what others do. You will get comfortable with what God says and does through you. Remember, God is about to do His greatest work through you and for you. It is so and so it is. There is nothing that the enemy can do about it.

Do you get our meaning here? God has already provided for you in everything. God sees ahead and has already taken care of it all. He has taken care of everything. Be encouraged, and have a wonderful Jesus-filled day. Get up and get out of that slumber, stupor, and out of that despair!

Know that God is with you and has already provided for every need and remember that for every need there is a Kingdom Answer.

REFLECT

Now that you are "warmed up," pick another new thing to try or do. Stretch yourself. Find new ways to be a blessing!

....
....
....
....
....
....
....
....
....
....
....
....
....
....
....

GIVE US THIS DAY OUR DAILY BREAD

NOTES

SWEET INSPIRATIONS

CHAPTER 3
Sitting

Sitting is so simple and yet, when you really think about it, it really is a rather dangerous "activity," because sitting has the potential to make you miss your moment, lose your drive, and direct your spiritual momentum to fall off the ledge! Sitting, sometimes, just happens to be the wrong posture for us to adopt. Sitting can sap our vitality, our energy. We find ourselves drifting into a place of complacency and for all the world we don't know how we got there! Most often, when you feel your energy level decrease, this loss of vitality comes simply from the position we call "sitting."

God positions us for His possession. Our lives are about living in His Kingdom so we want to keep our minds and our hearts on doing things that continually advance us in His direction. Sitting has a great tendency to take all of those ideas and inspirations away. Sitting down takes your advancement away and even thoughts of advancing right out of you. Sitting changes your state of mind out of reaching your potential or finding your fulfillment. We become complacent. We become too familiar with relaxation and instead of finding fulfillment we find ourselves just sitting in a stupor!

God wants us to shake that off! He needs us to shake that off! He wants us to understand that while we are here on earth we are to advance His Word, make progress on His behalf, and we are not to be hindered.

> God the Father continually gives us the *ability, the power, and the impetus* to push ahead in His Word.

So, the question now is, "Who hindered you?" "What hindered you?" "Why did you allow this to prevent you from moving forward in the Kingdom?" God the Father continually gives us the ability, the power, and the impetus to push ahead in His Word. One thing I've learned recently is when God said, "Let there be…" that it came into existence, it happened right then, right that second. So, now I want you to go back and study the word "be" and rediscover the position God needs you to "be" in.

When we talk about the word "be," we are talking about a very powerful word. The word "let," also contains a lot of strength. Let's do some homework this week, research the phrase "Let there be..." and discover what it actually means. "Let there be..." does not mean to just sit there. No way. "Let there be..." means to advance in four areas. We are going to advance in four areas and it is delightfully surprising to learn about the phrase "Let there be..."

REFLECT

Look up and write down the definition for the words "let" and "be." What position does God need you to "be" in?

....
....
....
....
....
....
....
....
....
....
....
....
....
....

When God said, "Let there be..." it was non-negotiable. Everything came into being immediately. So, when God speaks to us and tells us that our dreams, visions, and missions are coming to pass, He is not a man that He should lie. He not only tells us He is enabling us and equipping us, but He in fact combs all creation to come to our rescue and our assistance! God comes to do His bidding. It happens instantaneously and immediately.

We have to find where the gap is between when God speaks it, when we hear it, and when His Words manifest. Why is there a gap between any of these at all? We need to understand all of it is timing. There is something about the level of faith we have when God says a thing, that it is already done. However, some of us fall into moping, into a stupor, and end up in despair because we say, "I don't see manifestation..."

> If you can *see it* then *it is so!*

But you have seen manifestation. You have to get a glimpse of it by your faith. You'll see it by faith and when you begin to see it by faith it is happening. If you can see it then it is so! If you can see it, it is already done! Amen and Alleluia!

Begin right now, to get a picture, a glimpse of who you really are and where you are really going. Keep that image before you. I want you to become, to be, to just be.

SITTING

REFLECT

What is God showing you about who you really are?
Capture all of the details He is showing you.

Determine in your own soul that God has said, for you, "to be."

Understand you and I will just "be" that. Hear that again: **You just "be" that.**

"Be," goes back to our ancestors, all the way back to our historical beings, all the way back to our African being when it was said, "It is so." Understand, we are not talking Ebonics or bad grammar. We are not talking about merely existing. We are talking about being and living in the power of God. We are talking about living life in fullness, abundance, and the way God intends us to live. You will find in your research on "Let there be..." that God had everything about you already included into existence and on His Mind. He had every fine detail about you already determined and it is already done! You are going to get very excited!

We are not going to just give out golden nuggets, but all of us are going to start digging out golden nuggets and understanding who God is to us and who we are to Him. Our wonderful, dazzling relationship with Him really works! God is determined to bless you. He is determined that your life be a blessing to all the families of the earth and that His covenant with Abraham is still intact. He has determined, from the beginning of time, that your name is

> *God is determined to bless you.*

SITTING

going to be great, you will do great things, and He is even going to take care of your descendants.

REFLECT

Re-read what you journaled yesterday.
What parts of your personality support who God showed you who He made you to be?

....
....
....
....
....
....
....
....
....
....
....
....
....
....
....
....
....
....

Some things we worry about and occupy our minds are the very things preventing us from getting to manifestation. I hear the Lord say, "Obtain your healing and your deliverance," so we need to begin, right now, to think and be like God. Be just like God.

We also need to make powerful confessions every day. I want to share with you some confessions I made recently. Each day, I make confessions according to His Word. So, here are a few and maybe you will catch the verses; but I want you to know you need to make confessions every day. In this way, we make the power of His Word come into operation in our life. This is very significant for those of us who are believers. This is a very powerful and necessary part of our everyday lives; not just because of a particular holy season, but because of who we are in God and the direction in which we want to go.

SITTING

CONFESSIONS

- I, the Lord which sanctify you, am holy… (Lev. 21:8)
- The Lord, our Passover Lamb (Lev. 23)
- The Lord, our Jubilee – Lord, I enjoy freedom and liberty through you. (Lev. 25:10)
- The Lord, our Kinsman Redeemer – Lord, you are my Brother and You have redeemed me. (Lev. 25:25)
- The Lord is not a man that He should lie or the son of man that He should repent. He will bring to pass what He says. Lord, I can trust and stand on Your word. (Numbers 23:19)
- The Lord, a Star. Lord, shine Your light in my life. (Num. 24:17)
- The Lord, a Scepter. Lord release your power and authority in my life. (Num. 24:17)
- The Lord, a consuming fire. Consume the wicked with Your fire. (Deut. 4:24)
- The Lord, our God, is one Lord. There is only one God, and it is You, Lord. (Deut. 6:4)
- The Lord, who is to be loved with the whole heart. I love you with my whole heart. (Deut. 6:5)
- The Lord, who gives power to get wealth. I receive power to get wealth. (Deut. 8:18)

This sounds so simple, what we are doing, but that is the power of confession. We have begun to learn some truths and think about some of the developmental steps in the process for a victorious and prosperous life. When we make a confession we gain access and the ability to speak our new and victorious life into existence. This all comes about through the power and purpose of confession.

REFLECT

Go back and read these confessions out loud. Which ones touched your spirit? Were there any that you had a hard time believing? Visit that scripture in your Bible and journal what you find when you read The Word.

SITTING

See how simple it is to change the whole world around you with the words you release from your mouth? Remember, we become what we say, what we speak, and what we believe. Therefore, we absolutely must keep the Word of God ever before us, ever present within us, meditating upon it, and speaking it aloud. When we engage in this part of our mission we begin to create a new world.

> We become what we *say*, what we *speak*, and what we *believe*.

Why is this important? The world was framed by a Word from the Mouth of God. Do you not know that when we begin to hear God speak in Genesis, He had to create a language and that, before then, He had not spoken? Before then, we had not heard Him speak. He was creating a language we could understand. That was the beginning of something powerful, called "a word," and "a language."

I get so fascinated and excited when I delve into these scriptures. I want to pass that excitement on to you because it does change your life! When God talks about, "In the beginning…" He is really talking about the beginning, because He began to create a language so that He could have communication with His people. He needs to communicate with His creation. In the beginning, he wanted to communicate with creation and He wanted

SITTING

to create so, he began speaking a language never spoken before. He created it.

You have that same power, energy, and empowerment my friends. We talk about this all the time on *Sweet Inspirations*—using everything God has given into our hands. We live here on this earthly realm made in His likeness and His image! We are to be just like Him.

As for us, well, we are not sitting down. We remain serious about advancing the Kingdom. Together, we are moving forward and taking quantum leaps. This ministry is about individual advancing. Sometimes, we come together to celebrate this one or that one, but God in Heaven

> *He celebrates* each and every one of us *individually*.

wants you to know He celebrates each and every one of us individually. He alone is the reason we get up out of our seats and advance. He takes us right out of that sitting position, that state of stupor and despair, and causes all of us to move out. He ignites the flame that burns within us, our zeal, our passion to get up and get moving in His Word.

I know in my heart you have been inspired with this new part of your mission and you now have your own "Let there be…" to attend to.

SWEET INSPIRATIONS

REFLECT

Remember, these are devotionals that God has designed to get you up and moving; not to sit down and stop moving. Now is the time to get up, move out and advance.

SITTING NOTES

SWEET INSPIRATIONS

CHAPTER 4
Give Thanks to the Lord Always!

This is a wonderful time to be alive in the Kingdom. We have been called by God to give thanks to Him—continually. Today, our scripture is Ephesians 5:18–20 and it reads,

> *"Do not be drunk in wine which leads to debauchery. Instead, be filled with the Spirit. Speak to one another with psalms, hymns, and spiritual songs. Sing, and make music in your heart to the Lord, always giving thanks to God the Father for everything in the name of our Lord Jesus Christ."*

There must be a big deficit of thanksgiving for God to have this on His mind. You might be surprised at how many people receive the blessings of the Lord, or blessings from

God. You would definitely be surprised at the deficit where thanks and praise is concerned. Simply saying, "Thank you," and telling God, "Thank you," and we love Him, and how much we adore Him, and how much we appreciate Him simply does not do it. This does not do it at all, my friends.

You may remember the story of The Ten Lepers. Leprosy is a dreadful disease. If you suffer from leprosy, you have terrible sores all over your body, a fever, and you live in constant pain. In ancient times, some people were believed to have suffered the disease because they had displeased God somewhere along the line.

> We have been called by *God to give thanks* to Him— *continually*.

Jesus was on his way to Jerusalem when the ten lepers met up with him. The lepers kept their distance because the law required a leper to call out, "Unclean!" and stay a good distance away from other people.

The lepers called out, "Jesus, Master, have mercy on us!" because they had heard Jesus had cured people and they needed a miracle. Jesus told them to go and show themselves to the priests. As they went on their way, God sent down a miracle. The ten lepers instantly became clean and free of every aspect of this dreaded disease! Nine of the men continued on to see the priests but only one, a

GIVE THANKS TO THE LORD ALWAYS!

Samaritan, a foreigner, came back to thank Jesus personally. He was praising God in a loud voice and he fell at Jesus' feet thanking Him. Jesus told the Samaritan, "Rise and go. Your faith has made you well."

This parable speaks to us across the ages—across all space and time. We might consider that today, with the world being much the same as it was 2,000 years ago, it is still a fairly accurate estimate that only ten percent of us today, one out of every ten, truly give God the praise or thanksgiving that we should be giving Him.

So let's change those statistics right now! We don't belong to that ten percent. Let us thank God constantly for all the mercies He has bestowed and showered upon us all of our lives. Let us increase the number of the thankful, the faithful. We—you and I, must increase.

REFLECT

Write a prayer of thanksgiving. Think of the blessings of God – both big and small.

....

....

....

....

....

....

SWEET INSPIRATIONS

GIVE THANKS TO THE LORD ALWAYS!

The Greek word for thanksgiving is "Eucharistia." The heart of that word is "charis" meaning "grace." Therefore, the heart of "eucharis" is "grace" and the heart of "charis" is "chairo" which means "to rejoice." "Thanksgiving," then, means

> "...to rejoice in God's presence for blessings we have freely received from Him."

Thanksgiving is a joy expressed in words and deeds toward God for His grace in word and in deed. Let's agree to not just say it but that we are going to truly feel a fullness of gratefulness in our hearts. We are going to be grateful for God and to God because He **has** done great things for us.

The song says, "He has done great things—bless His Holy Name." So giving thanks flows in abundance only from the heart of a spirit-filled believer.

> *Giving thanks flows in abundance only from the heart of a spirit-filled believer.*

Listen well; we cannot be found acting like unbelievers and not giving God thanks.

The spirit-filled person is constantly reminded of God's goodness. Another song says, "Every time I think of the goodness of Jesus, it makes a praise come up, it gives you joy; it gives you peace and happiness." You just cannot help but thank our powerful and good God. Today, tell someone you cannot help but thank and praise God. That's just how good He's been to us.

REFLECT

Write another prayer of thanksgiving – without repeating anything from yesterday's prayer.

....
....
....
....
....
....
....
....
....
....
....
....
....
....
....
....
....

GIVE THANKS TO THE LORD ALWAYS!

Let's look further: "For although they knew God, they glorified Him not as God nor gave thanks to Him." That is not the group to be in folks! We are in the group called, "...he that believeth and he that giveth thanks." Not only that, we are also in the group called, "...he that giveth thanks to the Lord always." We are going to be found rejoicing in the God of Our Salvation, always.

We look to II Chronicles 20 which talks about King Jehoshaphat who was facing some serious trouble. Some men came and told Jehoshaphat, "...a vast army from across the sea is coming up against you." Jehoshaphat was frightened. He hastened to talk to God, to pray. He prayed before all of the people, saying he knew, and the people knew, how powerless they were against their enemies. And when Jehoshaphat had finished his prayers the Spirit of the Lord spoke through Zechariah's son, Jahaziel. And the Spirit of the Lord said to not become afraid or to lose heart because this was not their battle.

This was God's battle!

The Lord told them to go into battle with their enemy in the morning at the edge of the wilderness but that they would not have to fight! God said, "Take your places, stand firm, and see how the LORD will be with you to deliver you. Do not fear or lose heart."

Jehoshaphat fell to the ground in thanks, just like the one leper who came back. And all of Jehoshaphat's people fell to the ground in thanksgiving like he did.

In the morning, as they were going out to meet the enemy, Jehoshaphat reminded them about what the LORD had said. He appointed some of the people to sing the praises of God and he sent them to the front lines! And the moment they began to sing, **the MOMENT they began to sing,** the LORD laid an ambush on Jehoshaphat's enemies from some other people of the enemy line! And they ended

> "Take your places, *stand firm,* and see how the LORD will be with you to deliver you. *Do not fear or lose heart.*"

up exterminating each other! There were no survivors.

Jehoshaphat and his people moved to take the plunder of battle. They found an abundance of cattle, garments, precious vessels, and personal property. The spoils were so great, it took Jehoshaphat and his men three days to gather them. On the fourth day they held an assembly to bless and thank the LORD for all he had done for them. And the fear of God came upon all the surrounding lands when they heard how the LORD had fought against the enemies of Israel. Thereafter, Jehoshaphat's kingdom enjoyed peace.

Listen, children, we are just like Jehoshaphat. We do not have any power at all to face the enemy attacking us.

GIVE THANKS TO THE LORD ALWAYS!

However, this is God's battle.

He has the power. We have to remember only one thing—all the power in the universe is in God's hands. Without Him, we don't know what to do. We don't even know where to begin.

We do need to keep our eyes upon Him and thank Him and praise him.

REFLECT

Think of a time when you could have praised and thanked the Lord for something but chose not to do it. It's not too late! Write your thanks and praise now!

....
....
....
....
....
....
....
....
....
....
....
....

SWEET INSPIRATIONS
NOTES

GIVE THANKS TO THE LORD ALWAYS!

SWEET INSPIRATIONS

CHAPTER 5
Watch and Pray (Agrupneo)

What a glorious day in The Kingdom. Recently, we were in Nanuet, NY and we kicked off our evangelical service. I tell you God came in great demonstration and we saw and felt great awe and wonder in that place. We had a great worship service, too. I cannot think of a word in the dictionary to describe what is happening in the northeast area here but we have seen something really sensational. God sent us there on assignment and we hold services there Friday and Sunday nights at 7:30PM. People are being healed and delivered. This is not hearsay or a cliché. We don't just say things. This has become the real deal.

So this got me to thinking on a word from the ancient Greek and I want to share it with you: Agrupneo which means "...to watch and pray." We need to watch the world news so we can keep up with what is going on. We need to pay close attention to current events so we may become more fully aware of the fulfillment of prophecy. I hope each and every one of us has kept up with what has been happening in Israel and we are praying for them. We must make absolutely certain we are watching as well as praying. God calls us to the wall, but the Greek word, "Agrupneo," translates "to watch." Agrupneo means to remain sleepless, to keep awake, and it refers to our spiritual person. **Right now is not the time to sleep.** It is not the time for our spiritual person to go into slumber. We need to activate, deepen, and maintain a sharp alertness.

> We must make absolutely certain we are *watching* as well as *praying*.

REFLECT

What are you doing to be on watch? What situations in the world today really touch your spirit? Write our prayers, using scriptures for those people.

....
....
....
....
....

WATCH AND PRAY (AGRUPNEO)

The Book of Luke 21:36 says, "Be always on the watch, and pray, that you may be able to escape all that is about to happen, and that you may be able to stand before the Son of Man." These are not scare tactics, folks; this is real. This passage lets us know **God has placed us here on Earth on purpose and He has placed us here to rule, to reign, and to have dominion.** He has placed us in charge; He has delegated authority to us. We become the ones who sit on the wall and determine what comes and what goes. All of us, everywhere around the world, need to increase our watchfulness. The New American Standard Bible translation reads, "But keep on the alert at all times…" Listen, we do not even have time to let our guard down. We do not have time to stop and smell the roses; we do not have time to be distracted. We do not have the time we might think we have; because really, we just don't have the time we used to have. It's time to give wasting time the big, "Time Out." We cannot use "wasted" time. We have to know exactly what time it really is, and wake up.

> We do not *have time* to be *distracted*.

Last night, the Holy Ghost kept saying "It is time for Me to demonstrate My glory." So, there are going to be some things that are going to transpire. We are going to have

WATCH AND PRAY (AGRUPNEO)

to be alert; bring closure to those things that need closure and we need to become aware of what is on the Mind of God for us—and what is on God's Mind for us right now. We are in for some events that are going to astound the world because God is the One who allows certain things to unfold until we cry out, "Holy!" God does not look for the sinner to cry out so much; but He looks for those of us who call ourselves believers. Those of us who say we are His children, those of us who are called His sons and His daughters, we are the ones He wants to hear cry out to Him. God wants to hear our voices. He is listening for a certain sound in the earthly realm that only we can give.

REFLECT
What things in your life do you need to bring closure to so you can be alert?
Ask God what is on His mind for you.

....
....
....
....
....
....
....
....

SWEET INSPIRATIONS

WATCH AND PRAY (AGRUPNEO)

We need to get excited because **God needs every one of us.** When you can still hear that God has need of you, then you have heard something that is most powerful and awesome, because whatever He wants to accomplish He can only accomplish it through you and me. That is why we are still here, folks. We bring Him glory and honor. We are here to give Him thanksgiving so all of us need to be on high alert. We need to know when that thermostat has gotten low on giving thanks, worship, and praise. And we all need to keep those thermostats as high as we can possibly set them. We need for our levels to continually rise every day. God needs us to increase and intensify, so we need to watch and we need to pray.

REFLECT

Where is your thermostat on giving thanks? Worship? Praise? What are some of your "go to" praise and worship music? Search for some new songs to shift and increase your praise and worship.

....
....
....
....
....
....

SWEET INSPIRATIONS

WATCH AND PRAY (AGRUPNEO)

It amazes me that some say, "Pray that you may be able to escape...," or, "Pray that you may have strength," and "Pray that you be strong enough." Listen to the English Standard Version: *"...but stay awake at all times praying."* The New Living Translation reads, *"Keep alert at all times and pray."* Listen, regarding this watch and pray thing; I say these are our survival instructions. God has left earth and Jesus has left us with some survival instructions. Be ready! The New Century Version says: "Be ready all the time; pray that you will be strong enough..." The Amplified Bible says: "Keep awake then and watch at all times [be discreet, attentive and ready] praying you may have the full strength and ability and be counted worthy to escape all these things [taken together] that will take place, and to stand in the presence of the Son of Man."

> He is *going to continue* to do what He's always done:
> take *care* of us,
> *watch* over us,
> and *bless* and *keep* us.

Isn't that interesting? It begins with, "Keep awake," then continues with "and watch at all times," [be discreet, attentive and ready]; and finally the last part of the command reads, "to stand in the presence of the Son of God, to be counted worthy, to escape all these things."

God has sent His Divine Protection, folks, and all He needs for us to do is to continue to do what He's called us to do. We are here in this earthly realm to give Him glory, praise, and thanksgiving. He is going to continue to do what He's always done: take care of us, watch over us, and bless and keep us. We surely owe Him thanksgiving because look around you—we are all still here! We have seen storm after storm raging; tropical storms, hurricanes, floods, we have seen it all. We have seen raging, towering fires in the forest.

After everything, after all of it, we are still here. We are here and we owe Him praise and thanksgiving!

REFLECT

List out the storms He has brought you through. Write a prayer of praise and thanksgiving. What specifically has God called you to do while in His Divine protection?

....
....
....
....
....
....
....
....

WATCH AND PRAY (AGRUPNEO)

Doesn't it amaze you the enemy is still trying? It amazes me. He has to try, but we know the Bible says, "No weapon that is formed against you is going to prosper." I want you to get your mind on track and gather it up because God is going to use you, whether you believe it or not. God is going to use you and He is going to throw open some doors this week. He makes "someway," out of "no way." He is going to make some crooked paths straight because He has placed us here to have dominion and we need to be ruling and reigning. That means that we are going to have to be on alert. We are going to have to do those two things that He's telling us right now. We are going to have to watch as well as pray. We must get our spirit person continually in that state where he is always watching and praying.

> We are going to have to *watch* as well as *pray*.

We are about to see what God has been telling us about this great outpouring and this great time of deliverance and this great healing that has come upon the land. I think of the power we saw with Hurricane Sandy; but Sandy was no match for the power of our God. I think how God is now about to bless you will make Hurricane Sandy look elementary, because God is going to show forth His power and His glory. And the way that He is going to do it is in the magnitude of the manifestations of the blessing that He has called forth into your life and upon your life.

Today, I just want you to walk around and say, "Even me. God is blessing me. He has not forgotten me." At a service recently, one of the most wonderful, inspiring things happened. I called down a young lady. She had gray hair and she was sitting sort of far from me. But the Holy Ghost inspired me to look in her direction. So, I called her down. Someone told me she could not speak English. She spoke only Spanish. I said, "I can tell you this Holy Ghost is universal." When that woman came down, the Holy Ghost had me tell her, "Jesus loves you! Jesus loves you! Jesus loves you!" and the power of God went into demonstration, and slew her in the spirit, and I am telling you she was so grateful. She was so grateful and I could understand what she was saying. She came by me after the service and she was still weeping. She was so, so grateful God had spoken to her and told her that He loved her; that He loved her with the greatest of love.

Jesus loves you and He loves you with the greatest of love, and with a greater love than that. You don't have to sit there and feel down and out—whatever the current

> *Jesus loves you* and He loves you with the *greatest of love!*

circumstances are. You can move directly into a state of celebration because you most definitely can celebrate God for something. You are alive and well in The Kingdom today. Listen, God is blessing His people. I am laughing and I have my hand up right now and I want to take a victory lap in this hotel where I am writing to you, but I can't do that in this little room! I want everyone to know that right now, I hear an FYI which says, "Seize your opportunity to give Him thanks." Make sure you don't miss your opportunities to give Him thanks and to be a witness unto Him and for Him in the earth realm today.

REFLECT

"Even me. God is blessing me. He has not forgotten me." Speak that out loud several times. As you receive the love of Jesus, journal your praise and thanksgiving.

....
....
....
....
....
....
....
....

WATCH AND PRAY (AGRUPNEO)

Let's get out there and let's turn this world upside down because Jesus…I heard that old song that says, "Jesus said it; Jesus said it." And when He said it, you can bank on it. It is so and so it is. He is going to do the phenomenal and greater still! We need to expect He is going to do even greater than this and greater than that.

I hear that FYI again. God wants to do much more than He has ever done before.

Will we let Him?
Yes, we will!
Will we invite Him in?
Yes, we will!
Will we welcome Him?

> *It is so and so it is.*

Yes, we will! I told a group recently that the correct response is always, "Yes, we will. Yes, we are going to do it and we are going to obey." I was giving them the scenario of the fishermen on the boat Jesus used. Simon said, "Master we have toiled all night. We haven't caught anything. Nevertheless, at your word, I will do it. I will launch out and I will throw this net. I am going to throw these nets, at Your word."

People, it is imperative we take God at His Word. Those words "watch and pray" are survival instructions. Your next survival instruction is "At Thy Word, I will do it." It doesn't make any sense. It doesn't add up. It isn't logical but because of the Word of God, the Word you have received,

WATCH AND PRAY (AGRUPNEO)

we are going to do it. We are going to obey. We have to obey. When we obey, that is when we are going to live from the glory, live from the realm we have never lived before and in a dimension that we've never been before. We have to remain obedient. We have to remain watchful and we have to remain prayerful. These are survival instructions and whatever we hear the Father say to do, we need to get to it and right away!

REFLECT

We have to remain watchful, prayerful, and obedient; and then say **"Yes, I will!"**

At this time in your life, what do you think is God's intended purpose for you here in the earthly realm?

....
....
....
....
....
....
....
....
....
....

Sweet Inspirations

WATCH AND PRAY (AGRUPNEO)

Get ready, because God is faithful to His Word. He gave me a prophetic song this weekend and the words are, "I will, I will do it; I will, I will." Then He says, "I make a promise, I promise you I will."

Whatever it is that you believe God for today, He says in response to your situation and to your needs, He will, He will do it and He will perform. Not only did He say that, He also said I make the promise, I make the promise to you. And the second verse says, "You will see it; you will see it". And He says here, "I promise, I make this promise. I make this promise to you. You will see it. You will see Me demonstrate My power and My glory on your behalf!"

That is enough to scream for, folks! Not only is He going to do it, you will see it. Abraham walked and walked and walked for miles, put up the tent, took down the tent, and he was called the father of the faith. He walked but he never saw it with his natural eye. He saw it by faith. However, I am telling you that you will see manifestation; you are going to see it and He says He will, and He promises. He promises you today He will do it and that you will see it. That's enough to give Him glory and thanks.

> We give *God glory* and *praise.*

What God is working on for us is a formula for life

where we are giving Him glory and thanksgiving 365 days of the year. Every time we think about Him, we need to be telling him, "Thanks!" We need to be giving Him praise and thanksgiving! Hallelujah! We give God glory and praise. We have so much to give Him thanks for.

Remember we are to watch and pray at all times. To God be the Glory!

REFLECT

As you are walking by faith, what manifestations are you seeing in the natural? What manifestations are you seeing by faith?

....

....

....

....

....

....

....

....

....

....

....

....

WATCH AND PRAY (AGRUPNEO)

NOTES

SWEET INSPIRATIONS

Chapter 6
Gratitude is the Way to Success

When we find ourselves in the month of November, we here at *Sweet Inspirations* focus on giving God praise and thanksgiving for each of the 30 days of the month. But when you meditate on it, you realize this is a way of life and that it should be going on 365 days of the year. **Every day is Thanksgiving Day for us.**

Gratitude is the way to success and the way of success. We do not ask God for anything. We only give thanks! Understand—this particular thing that we undertake, for lack of a better word, draws us ever closer to God, and you need to write that down. We need this every day. We need to get closer to God.

The second thing we need to understand about a month

of thanksgiving is following a month of thanksgiving is a lot of miracles. After doing this nonstop for a month, you can expect the phenomenal and the miraculous. God does not let this go unnoticed and unrewarded. This is what He has had on His heart forever. There is purpose and reason for this. We need to get our expectancy up because He has told us we can never expect anything less than a miracle. Now is the right time for us to focus on our personal praise and our personal worship to God. We need to sharply focus in on that. Sometimes you will see a lot of philanthropic activity and a lot of "one time out of the year" activity when the holidays come in. We start giving to others because that is foremost in our minds. We start looking for people to bless.

That is supposed to be the attitude we have all year long. This is gratitude; we return the favor and bless those and we bless others because God has been so good to us. He has done so much for us. I am telling you also that the future is bright, so we give Him thanks for what He is about to do. We stand in awe of God because He has pulled off some stuff that was beyond us and that we had no control over. If He had not done it, we don't know where

> *The future is bright, so we give Him thanks for what He is about to do.*

we would be right now. But God is so good and so faithful that He delivered, He healed, He set free; He came at the right time and on time, and He came with the goods, folks. We need to praise Him and lift up those holy hands and we need to be giving Him the fruit of our lips. This thing is serious. It is as if God has us in a time capsule, a bubble, or an incubator; and He is feeding off of the praises and the worship that is coming up from the earth realm in this hour! He does not let it go unnoticed or unrewarded. Praise is the bloodstream and heartbeat of God. Singing your praise for Him gets His attention. He zeros in on this for this very hour. He has planned something great for the Kingdom. We need to understand He not only blesses His Kingdom, but we need to be Kingdom-minded in this hour.

REFLECT

Honestly, how would you rate yourself on a scale of 1-10 for your gratitude towards God?
Why do you give yourself that ranking?
What will you do to increase your rating?

....
....
....
....
....
....

SWEET INSPIRATIONS

GRATITUDE IS THE WAY TO SUCCESS

The question arises this morning, "Why are we not great, or doing great, in the Kingdom of God?" Well, for one thing most churches or church people have become lackadaisical. The spirit of procrastination has crept up into the church and I am not talking about a building. I am talking about a people. **To live in God means for us to work on developing ourselves every single second of our lives.** I want to talk about that because we spend a lot of time getting ourselves ready for this world's system; but we need to be developing ourselves and maturing spiritually for the Kingdom at hand. We grow physically and we need to be growing in stature spiritually. One reason we are not seeing great things in the Kingdom and not doing great things in the Kingdom is because of that dismal spirit we have allowed to penetrate our very beings! We cannot be passive in praise and giving thanks. That's what I want to say right now. We cannot be passive in praise, worship, thanksgiving and prayer. We cannot give ourselves permission to be passive. As a matter of fact, we need to get as assertive as we can. As I always say, the enemy has intensified his strategy, so we need to intensify our strategy.

> We cannot be passive in *praise, worship, thanksgiving* and *prayer.*

REFLECT

Write this down: **"To live in God means for us to work on developing ourselves every single second of our lives."**

....
....
....
....
....

What is your strategy for being intentional about praise?

....
....
....
....
....
....
....
....
....
....
....

GRATITUDE IS THE WAY TO SUCCESS

We have become so accustomed to going to church, and having friends and relations at church. A lot of us do not skip even one major church event, but that is not because we are trying to get close to God. It is because church has become a part of our subculture and we simply, continually go. What we say to people is that we are not to overload ourselves. We are not to expose ourselves. We do a minimum of work and we find many reasons why it is impossible to complete tasks God has given us. Understand, God will not force us. However, we need to choose wisely on what we focus on, what our priorities need to be, and what is vital for us to have godly success, become great in the Kingdom, and do great deeds in the Kingdom. That takes discipline, people, and we are going to have to spend quality time worshiping and praising, in prayer, in fasting, and in consecration.

We have to go the *distance*

We must get away quickly from doing just enough to stay afloat. We have to go the distance and rebuke that passive spirit. We have to destroy it! We have to go the distance. We want to see God in His glory and in His great demonstration of His power. We have to buckle down and say to ourself, "Self, you are going to praise, you are going to worship, you are going to pray, you are going to give thanksgiving, and you are going to give it and love it and give it with a cheerful heart! You're going to be obedient like you know you need to be obedient in order to see the Kingdom of God advance-advance-advance! The Kingdom of God has to remain foremost in our hearts, minds, and spirits. I am here to tell you one thing and you know it is true.

Everything we have belongs to the Lord.

Here is a reason to be thankful. I've been looking at this recently, because I have been at a hospital facility visiting with my mom for the last few days. I have been looking at those who are sitting there. They have come to a closing stage in their physical lives. Most are in their 80's or 90's. Some folks have survived into their 100's.

They are there, but they are not there.

So, we need to be thankful God is keeping us, and every day we get up we need to declare prophetically, and receive His benefits and His power to stay in our right minds, to continually remain active and use our limbs!

REFLECT

Think about your body and your mind. List out the ways God has kept you in your mind and body.

....

....

....

GRATITUDE IS THE WAY TO SUCCESS

This is major, people. Do you really think in your heart of hearts that the enemy will play fair with you? Uh-uh. No. Not gonna happen. EVER. Everything that comes out of your mouths counts! You cannot afford to be walking around talking about, "I'm about to lose my mind," "I'm so tired," "My whole body's about to break down."

Stop talking like that. I'm speaking as a mom here, because whatever you are saying is going to happen and what you are going to experience. That is the principle of the Word of God. You need to understand the power of your words. So, there is power in thanksgiving, there's power in praise, there is power in worship. That is what should be foremost and coming out of our mouths, coming out of our very being; the very essence of our being. We need to be active, assertive, progressive agents of worship, praise, and thanksgiving. This is our role because it grants the

> We become *active* when we *assert* ourselves in Him.

Spirit of God greater access and greater entrance into the earthly realm. We become active when we assert ourselves in Him. When we make ourselves into agents of worship, praise, and thanksgiving, we experience the Kingdom of

GRATITUDE IS THE WAY TO SUCCESS

God advancing like never before! Every day there can be miraculous activity in the earthly realm because of our praise and worship. You had better get ready.

REFLECT

Watch your words. Are there sayings you are using that could be used against you?

What sayings can you use instead?

Listen, there is no time now for us to be shirking our responsibilities or side-stepping away from the plate. We must assume those leadership roles God calls us to. We have to become more active and our motives have to be pure in going to church and for serving our brothers and sisters. This is not the time to say, "I'm getting ready to establish myself and I will be discovered and I will achieve my goal." You must understand, your motive has to be pure. No longer can you have the idea that you are going to 'squeeze' yourself through and "manage to keep your head above water." I tell you this. We have to get our motives straight and we need to do that before we enter into a new realm. Let's make sure our hearts are right and fixed. Then, we need to make sure our mind is made up and we are in this thing for the long haul and that we are going the distance. **We are about to get assertive, progressive, and active where our praise, our prayer, our worship, and our thanksgiving are concerned.** It is a continual and a perpetual flow and then the miracles are going to be a continual and a perpetual flow. Get ready for it. Get ready for an onslaught of positive activity in your life. That is the guarantee for success. Your thanksgiving guarantees the win even before the battle begins!

> Your *motive* has to be *pure*.

REFLECT

As a believer, we are all called to lead in our own special way. How and where is God calling you to lead? What are you committed to do to get more assertive?

SWEET INSPIRATIONS

Keep it going. Keep the fire going. Keep moving. Keep advancing. Keep progressing. This is continual.

Forever keep the Word of God in your ears and you will forever build your faith. Just as great as it is on God's mind to bless you and do the phenomenal for you, I want you to know God is building up your inner man; He's building up your faith level; He's building you in Him; He's building Himself up in you. You are becoming one; you're in sync; your mind is going to be His mind; your thoughts are going to be His thoughts. Your heart is going to be singing songs and hymns and praise and doing praise and worship and making melody. It is a constant flow now, because the miracles are going to be continual. Your praise, here on this forefront in America, can impact nations around the world. Nations are going to begin to see the benefits of those of us who have kept the mind of thanksgiving, kept the mind of Christ; kept the mind of praise and worship; they are going to begin to reap and give a harvest.

---

*He's building you in Him;
He building Himself up in you.*

GRATITUDE IS THE WAY TO SUCCESS

REFLECT

Reflect back on where you were in God 6 months ago, 1 year ago, 3 years ago. Praise God for the transformation He has made, what He is doing and what He is going to do!

....
....
....
....
....
....
....
....
....
....
....
....
....
....
....
....
....
....

I do not get weary in well-doing. We are not asking God for anything; we are thanking God. I'm thanking God for my mother's health; I'm thanking God my mother is back home; I'm thanking God! Listen, it is already done. You have to take your mind to the Mind of God and I want you to hang out there and if it is a thought that He didn't think, don't you think it. If it is a word that He didn't say, then don't you say it. Everything counts in this moment. I cannot stress this enough.

I say this as if it were the announcement of World War II, but this is World War and we have already won! This battle is already fought and won. The fight is fixed! This is already a done deal in the Holy Ghost and what we are about to receive are the goods and the bounty and the benefits for standing in the midst, staying on the wall, and being obedient. There is a great reward coming and there is a great reward in operation even right now. You need to stay focused. Don't be lured off the victory ground by the enemy. Don't you let him make you say those things that you know are not of God. Don't even think it; don't even sniff it. "As a man thinketh, so is he".

> There is a *great reward coming* and there is a great reward in *operation even right now.*

GRATITUDE IS THE WAY TO SUCCESS

We are concentrating on the goodness of God, the greatness of God, the awesomeness of God and we are concentrating on Him using us greatly in His kingdom. We are not backing down. We cannot back down. We move ahead. People, go to celebration and stay there and allow God to have His way. Today, we say "yes" to His will and to His way and we shall obey.

Some of you reading this may say, "I don't have a thing to celebrate." We need to remember that, if you are breathing, you have something to celebrate! You have something very precious to be thankful for. It may not have been as you had wanted it to be, but God is still good. It may not have happened quite the way you wanted it to, but God is still good. It may not have happened exactly when you thought it should have, but God is still good. With all of that, He is still faithful. He has spoken, and if He has said it, it shall surely come to pass. You can bank on that.

REFLECT

What are you celebrating? List our everything you can think of to celebrate with God.

....
....
....
....
....

SWEET INSPIRATIONS

GRATITUDE IS THE WAY TO SUCCESS

NOTES

SWEET INSPIRATIONS

CHAPTER 7
Every Space Must Be Filled With Praise

God is up to something where we are concerned. The best is yet to come and there is a breakthrough, a breaker anointing, resting over us. We give God the glory. We thank Him. Recently, at Redeeming Love Christian Center in Nanuet, New York, we had an amazing outpouring of phenomenal blessings, phenomenal miracles, and the phenomenal touch of the Lord. God is performing his miracles in the northeast region and most definitely in the Tri-state area. God is doing what He has promised to do.

> *God is doing what He has promised to do.*

Last night, we dealt with praise and God asked me in the early morning, in the wee, small hours, "What would happen if praise was absent? What would happen in the absence of praise?" I sat there for a moment and I understood where He was going. I said to Him, "Lord, in the absence of praise we are all the way back to Genesis Chapter 1, Verse 1! We are back to chaos, confusion, darkness, and void. We are moved back to the very beginning. We start over. He said these words to me: "The lack of praise causes barrenness and prevents the production of life. As far as the east is to the west, every state between the west and the east, the north and the south should be given to praising His Name."

> As far as the *east is to the west*, every state between the west and the east, **the north and the south** should be given to *praising His Name.*

The Book of Psalms 113:3 reads, "From the rising of the sun unto the going down of the same, the LORD's name is to be praised." Most people think that means from morning to night. That is one good scenario; it is good to think like that. Every moment should be filled with praise and every moment should be filled with thanksgiving. But

EVERY SPACE MUST BE FILLED WITH PRAISE

from the rising of the sun until the going down of the same means that the sun rises in the east and sets in the west and every nation in between, east and west, and every nation in between, north and south, God has a remnant of folks who are going to give His Name praise. He says we should be giving His Name praise from the rising of the sun until the going down of the same. Hallelujah! The Lord showed me last night that every space must be filled; it is not even dealing with time, but with space. Every space between east and west; and every space between north and south, God has assigned a praiser to be in that space. So, if God is talking to us about praising, and about giving Him thanksgiving, it is all because your praise and your thanksgiving has a purpose. We were created to praise and worship Him. I am still excited from last night!

> *You are a Praise Specialist*

What we talked about last night was the subject: "You are a Praise Specialist." For example, when you get ready to go to the eye doctor, you don't go to someone that is going to look at your foot. You go to someone who specializes in the eyes and will make a diagnosis and draw a conclusion and will work on a strategy with you about which way to go in order to handle your eye situation. So, for every calamity that comes upon the earth, for everything that happens in the earthly realm, God has a unique group He has assigned to praise, worship, and give thanksgiving, because your praise has power! We need to remember that. And every moment of the day from east to west and from north to south and in between, there should be thanksgiving and praise going up into the Heart of God.

REFLECT

You are a praise specialist - a person highly skilled in the specific field of praise. What is your favorite way to show Him praise? Singing, shouting, dance, a musical instrument or some other way? How do you plan to expand your praise for God?

....
....
....
....
....
....
....
....
....
....
....

EVERY SPACE MUST BE FILLED WITH PRAISE

Praise is "an act of worship or acknowledgment, of which the virtues or deeds of another are recognized and exalted." There is no one on earth or in the heavens that needs to be exalted or praised more than our God. The praise of men toward God is the means by which we express our joy to the Lord. We are to praise Him for who He is and what He does. So, in Psalms 113:2-3; we read, "Blessed be the Name of the LORD from this time forth and forever. From the rising of the sun to its setting, The name of the LORD is to be praised."

> *It is always a good time to praise.*

We need to remember that it is always a good time to praise. Verses two and three from Psalm 113 let us know it is indeed the right time to praise. In everything we do and in all times of the day we are to praise Him. Another reference to that is the Book of Malachi 1:11, " For from the rising of the sun even unto the going down of the same, My Name shall be great among the Gentiles; and in every place incense shall be offered unto My Name, and a pure offering: for My Name shall be great among the heathen, saith the LORD of hosts."

Let's stop right here. The nations are going to be affected from the praise you give from where you are right now, this very moment. All the nations of the world will be impacted. Think global. Think and meditate on the countries where

EVERY SPACE MUST BE FILLED WITH PRAISE

they persecute Christians and where they do not want to recognize our God. They have other gods. Those nations are experiencing deprivation and extreme poverty, and one crisis after another. They lack proper food, clothing, shelter, and even drinking water. In some places food is very scarce. When praise is void and absent, our lives are left void, empty and barren. We see that in many Third World developing countries. We need to understand and strengthen the fact that America is blessed because Christianity is strong here. At any given moment, we are folks who sincerely give God praise and glory. We have record numbers of prayer warriors, people seeking God, and those who really know their God. We are seeing major deeds accomplished in His Name. Those who diligently seek Him see the rewards and the benefits of seeking God.

REFLECT

Meditate on the people who are going to be affected by your praise. Ask God to show you specific countries, people and situations you will impact through your praise. Journal what He tells you.

....
....
....
....
....

SWEET INSPIRATIONS

EVERY SPACE MUST BE FILLED WITH PRAISE

The first point I want to make from our Psalm 113 is it says to praise Him in the good times. The good things happening for you come from God. Some people get confused because they think their money causes them to have a measure of comfort or prosperity. However, money is just a resource, it is not the source. The source is God. Our God is the source of the blessing. I don't care if it's a promotion or a bonus check. I don't care if your doctor decided differently in your favor on the results of a test. It didn't come from man. It all originated with God. He wants us, His people, to always remember, remember, remember—give Him the glory!

> It all *originated* with *God*.

The other night, I wrote this down and my team told me to read this on the air twice. I may have to type it twice here, as well.

We have to get to the place where we realize we are not getting ahead in life because of something we are doing, but rather, because of what God is doing around us, through us, and for us.

Amen and amen! Let's have that once more!

We have to get to the place where we realize we are not getting ahead in life because of something we are doing, but rather, because of what God is doing around us, through us, and for us.

SWEET INSPIRATIONS

REFLECT

Praise God in the good times. What good times are you experiencing right now? Praise Him!

EVERY SPACE MUST BE FILLED WITH PRAISE

The next point is that if we are to praise Him in the good times, we also need to praise Him in the bad times. When we go to the Book of Daniel, Chapter 6, we find this. Daniel did not let the government keep him from doing what he knew was right. Listen, don't let the government keep you from doing what you know is right. Don't let others dictate to you, influence you, and cause you to do wrong by God who stands by you, wakes you up, keeps you healthy, and in your right mind; who keeps a roof over your head, food on your table, clothes on your back; keeps your children safe; keeps you healed, gives you the activity of life and the use of your limbs. Don't sell Him short when it comes to praising Him, people. The Lord God is in control.

> Don't sell *Him* short *when* it comes to *praising Him*

Recently, the Lord spoke to me during our service and He urged me to physically walk around our building so that His Presence might release the power and the anointing to destroy illnesses! That is what we were doing the other night. He said to us that He had given us the ability through our praise to destroy the yokes and infirmities of diseases. And we canceled them out; we brought illnesses and disease to nothing last night. God destroyed them!

But that is nothing compared to what He is going to do for us who have been faithful and obedient to Him. Hallelujah! We destroy the yoke of the enemy and we lift the heavy burden. Chains fall off the lives of people around the world because we have decided to obey God and tell Him, "Yes!" All of this happens when we give Him thanksgiving without asking Him for anything.

REFLECT

What are the influences in your life that are tempting you to do wrong by God? What is it they are tempting you to do? Decree and declare, "I will praise God no matter what my circumstances or my situation!"

EVERY SPACE MUST BE FILLED WITH PRAISE

There is a powerful explosion coming upon the earthly realm and yes, there might be a calamity coming. But God said that when we praised Him and thanked Him, that would become our "preventive medication." Our praise and thanksgiving keeps us safe, out of harm's way, and our children out of harm's way. The Almighty said that calamity would come upon on the face of the earth but would not even come near our doors. We need for someone, right now, to just jump and skip like "Mary Had a Little Lamb," and although we are on these written pages and I cannot hear you right this second, this is a "Thank You, God," moment.

> But God said that *when we praised Him and thanked Him*, that would become our *"preventive medication."*

That's what happened at church the other night. We were having "Thank You, God," moments. We made sure every moment counted. We didn't miss a single one. Every time God gave us the Holy Ghost cue, we knew to get up and give God praise and glory. That's exactly how I am feeling right now. So, we need to get up right this second. Get up! Don't sit there in that stupor! You get up, shake yourself, and tell your body, "I command you to praise

EVERY SPACE MUST BE FILLED WITH PRAISE

> *We glorify Him* in the good and glorify Him in the bad! *Hallelujah!*

God!" It doesn't matter how you "think" it feels. We don't care how it feels, how it looks, what you say, or what you do. You take charge. God has delegated you His authority, and now, you stand up, look the enemy square in his face and say, "Take this, right here! I am commanding my body to praise God! You may have taken your best shot, but God is The One who has the last say. We glorify Him in the good and glorify Him in the bad!" Hallelujah!

Look at the Book of Daniel, Chapter 6. Daniel's opponents at work knew they could never out-compete him on the job. He was that good. King Darius was thinking of putting Daniel in charge of everything. His opponents knew the only way they could remove Daniel was to force him to choose between God and Darius. So, they passed a law saying Darius was the one to be worshiped and praised above all others for the next thirty days! Daniel was not about to change his custom of going home to kneel down and pray in the upper chamber, three times a day, facing Jerusalem, with the windows open for all to hear! Daniel didn't let the government keep him from doing what he knew was right. So, he continued to pray and uplift the name of God and God returned the favor that while Daniel was in the lion's den, He sent an angel to shut the lions' mouths, and Daniel was not harmed in any way. Hallelujah! So, you see, what was supposed to be a very bad day, God turned it around for Daniel. Daniel had a very good day, and in the end his opponents, his accusers, and their wives and children, were the ones who ended up having a pretty bad day in the lion's den.

REFLECT

Write about a time when God turned what should have been a very bad day into a very good day. Praise Him again for His goodness!

EVERY SPACE MUST BE FILLED WITH PRAISE

It is now turnaround time in the Kingdom of God. What the enemy meant for bad, God is turning around for good. At this very moment, someone reading this is getting some immediate miracles, some immediate responses, and some immediate favors. That is just the way it is, folks. It is praising time in The Kingdom and in the Body of Christ. I'm here to tell you, "Get your praise on, get your praise on, and get your praise on!" It's praising time in the Kingdom and I'm excited about what God is up to where you are concerned. I'm excited for you reading this! God has used this time to get us into a different lifestyle, and a mode of giving Him praise and thanks. Your testimonies will be great and unusually phenomenal. I'm here to tell you that you are the recipient and the beneficiary of this great move that is happening right here. It is praising time, folk. It is praising time. Do not let your life be a life absent of praise. Do not fall into that mode. There is a penalty for not praising and there is a penalty for being unwilling to praise.

In the Book of Malachi 2:2, it says "...for those who do not praise, I will curse your blessings." Can you imagine God doing that? In the Book of Deuteronomy, Chapter 28,

> It's *praising time* in *The Kingdom*

EVERY SPACE MUST BE FILLED WITH PRAISE 151

the list of curses is there for those who choose not to uplift His name and follow His commands. It is a pretty long list. Psalm 22:23 says, "Ye that fear the Lord, praise Him." Psalm 34: 1, "His praise shall continually be in my mouth." Psalm 35:18, "I will praise thee among much people."

God inhabits the praises of His people. He lives inside your praises and thanksgiving to Him. Psalm 113 reads, "Give us the reasons for praise." Verse 5 says, "...there is no one else like Him." Verse 6 says, "He knows what is going on in Heaven and on earth." Verse 7 says, "He raises up the poor," and ultimately verse 9 says, "He makes the barren women have children." The Lord is on our side, folk. He is reason for everything and deserving of our fervent praise forever and ever! Hallelujah and Amen!

REFLECT

Journal the miracles you are experiencing from your praise.

....
....
....
....
....
....
....
....

SWEET INSPIRATIONS

EVERY SPACE MUST BE FILLED WITH PRAISE

NOTES

SWEET INSPIRATIONS

CHAPTER 8
A Tribute

I woke up early recently and the Lord spoke these words to me. He said, "A Tribute." I want you to hear what I am saying about a tribute. I looked it up in the dictionary because I really wasn't sure exactly where this was going. But listen to this. And by the way, He's not talking about money so don't get scared. God is talking about giving honor where honor is due. It says in the Merriam-Webster dictionary that the definition of tribute is,

- a payment from one ruler or nation to another in acknowledgment of submission or as the price of protection;
- a gift, a testimonial, a compliment or the like, as due or in acknowledgment of gratitude or esteem;
- a stated sum or other valuable consideration paid by one sovereign or state, in acknowledgment of subjugation or the price of peace, security, protection or the like;

- gifts or service showing gratitude, respect or affection like a floral tribute.

Then, God reminded me we hear the word, tribute, all the time during the course of a year or sometime we hear that people are sponsoring a concert as a tribute to a certain musician or a certain cause. You may remember some time back when they tied yellow ribbons on the trees as a tribute to soldiers overseas. Sometimes we hear about countries who are paying tribute to other countries because they want to pay for peace and not have to go to war.

But I want all of you to know I'm tying this in with the Christmas season. Everyone wants gifts. Everyone gives gifts and sometimes we tell people during birthdays, celebrations, and other holidays celebrations that you have to think about the person receiving the gift. You don't give the person something you want, but something that they want; something valuable to them. What we have been doing in these devotional chapters of *Sweet Inspirations* is giving God what He wanted. We have met His requirements in thanksgiving, in praise and in worship. God wants and needs every reader to know that we, together, have been

> *God* is talking about *giving honor* where *honor is due.*

A TRIBUTE

paying Him tribute for His goodness, His greatness, His sovereignty, His love, and for His kindness. We have set these few chapters aside to just give thanksgiving that is, to Him, a testimonial of His goodness, His mercy, His greatness, and His awesome power. This is what we have been doing in these chapters—giving thanks. God requires and needs us to give Him thanksgiving. Not only that, even though we pay Him tribute for His goodness, we can't give Him enough praise and worship. He knows we can't out do Him. The Lord Himself is so phenomenal, it will blow our minds what He will do on behalf of His people; what He will do for every one of His children. This is a landslide victory; a breakthrough portion that has been released in your behalf; this is an outpouring of grace coming in your direction and is headed right through the year. The miracles and the blessings are going to follow us and they are going to overtake us throughout the year.

REFLECT

Reflect on the tribute you have paid to God. What would you like to add to the tribute you have already started?

....

....

....

....

....

SWEET INSPIRATIONS

A TRIBUTE

My friend, God has given us a jump-start. We are about to see soon a manifestation of glory that we could not foresee. We have given thanks and praise to Him and now we are going to see a manifestation. I want you to get ready to receive your manifestation and when you do, I wonder if you might email me those praise reports? I receive many messages from my Sweet Inspirations listeners but now, as we take these words to print, I know you, reading this right now, will begin to see miracles, great and small, made manifest in your life. When you witness them, let me know. This is all part of the plan where you are concerned. I'm going to be sharing them.

We are also going to hear from the prophets across the land. Listen, folks, this is the real deal and I want to say it like the young folks, "It's going down like this." God said that it's going to be a blowing of the mind experience. I promise when you begin to hear the reports of what God has already started, you are going to be astounded. You're going to have to turn aside and you're are going to have to look in God's direction; not because you're in a state of shock but because you're in such a state of awe.

> *God said* it's going to be a *blowing of the mind experience.*

You are going to realize that even in the time we have just given Him in these few chapters, it's not comparable to the miracles and the blessings and the breakthroughs and the promises and the prophecies that are going to be made manifest so soon in your life.

You have paid tribute here and I don't want you to let up on this blazing trail of giving thanks. I want you to increase it and I mean I want you to look the enemy in the face, and begin to praise God. Dance! Dance on the enemy's head! God is sovereign. He has chosen to bless His people in this hour, at this moment, and in this time. This is the season, folks. We are going to continue to give Him tribute because we appreciate Him. We really appreciate Him. Most people connect that appreciation with money and yes, that is one of the definitions. But what God is after today is your affection. He's after your praise. Can you imagine that every waking moment is a praise moment, a "lift your hands" moment, an "open your mouth and magnify His name," moment?

REFLECT

Increase your praise. Increase your affection towards God. How are you increasing your praise and tribute to God?

....

....

....

A TRIBUTE

That's what He is after. Every space between east and west; north and south is occupied by a praiser. We speak it into existence. Every waking moment is occupied by someone giving Him thanksgiving; someone telling Him, "Thank you Jesus," someone telling Him how much they love Him, how much they adore Him, how awesome, and how wonderful. Someone, somewhere, is thanking Him deeply from the bottom of their heart. Every space between north and south, east and west, we prophetically declare that a praiser now occupy that space. Get ready, folks. It sounds like Heaven on earth! He's being worshiped there in Heaven 24/7; the angels, the archangels, cherubim, and seraphim, are all worshiping Him and bowing down 24/7 and we are joining in! This is a combustible explosion! I see in the spirit that folk are going to be able to look at their bodies and ask, "What happened to the tumor?" They will declare, "My body has just straightened out! I'm no longer a cripple. I'm no longer weak. My blood count returned to normal!" You are going to hear these things. You're going to hear

> *Every space* between *north and south, east and west,* we prophetically declare that a *praiser now occupy that space.*

A TRIBUTE

how God miraculously brought people out of comas, how He saved folks from collisions that look like they should have lost their lives and they didn't get a scratch!

You had better get ready. God proves Himself, demonstrates His power and His glory because a few of His children have chosen to give Him praise, honor and glory. I want to clap my hands and run around my mom's place here in North Carolina and give Him glory. I'm expecting, I expect God; He's going to prove Himself beyond measure. There is going to be salvation, healing, and deliverance beyond measure; masses! What we do here is going to have international impact. Nations are going to be impacted by our sowing the seed of thanksgiving, praise, and worship.

REFLECT

Take a moment to meditate and journal on God's power and His glory and how you have seen it manifest on earth. Sow more seeds of thanksgiving, praise and worship!

....
....
....
....
....
....
....
....

SWEET INSPIRATIONS

A TRIBUTE

I hope and believe God, that this has become a lifestyle and a priority with those of you who read this. You can tell it, you can tell it; I am excited; because when God gives us a mandate, He also at the same time gives us the power to fulfill that mandate. All He asks us to do is give to Him our thanks. When He asks us to do something for Him and we obey, He comes to us with the blessings, the miraculous and the supernatural! What could not be done is done in the name of Jesus! We are giving Him the tribute. Some of you need to send flowers to your office with a note that reads, "This is our tribute to God for His goodness." Some of you need to put some banners and some plaques up. Everyone in the world is getting plaques for doing great things, but they can only do it because of the goodness of God. We are not going to be ashamed to proclaim the goodness of God! We are not going to be ashamed to give a testimony! We are not going to be ashamed to give Him praise and to give Him the tribute! I would love to hear your tribute to God! Please e-mail your story to me!*

> This is *our tribute to God* for *His goodness.*

*Mother Judy Hines' contact information can be found on page 8.

SWEET INSPIRATIONS

REFLECT

What is your testimony? Write out your tribute to God. It doesn't matter if it is 25 years old, we are still celebrating the goodness of God!

A TRIBUTE

We are going to call out these tributes, testimonies, and breakthroughs during the Sweet Inspirations program. God is still moving and He is still on the throne. He is still in control and He is still doing great things on behalf of you and me. I want to tell you right now your world is getting better. It just got better. I say it all the time—life just got better and I believe it! I believe it with every fiber of my being. Every time I say it, it gets better and better and better! Some of you need to start saying it and agreeing with Heaven that your life just got better! No weapon formed against you is going to prosper. God has seen to it that every fine detail of your life is taken care of. You don't have one failing moment or one moment where you are going down. Every moment you have is a thanking moment, a thanksgiving moment, a moment to give praise. That's what we have in Sweet Inspirations. Every moment counts; so every moment someone reads this should be filled with giving God the praise and glory! We give Him tribute and thank Him. Let me tell you a little bit why we thank Him. We thank Him for His peace, security, and protection. The list becomes infinite. Hallelujah! We owe it to Him,

> We thank Him for *His peace, security, and protection.* The list becomes infinite. *Hallelujah!*

folks! We have not just had rumors of wars, we have lived through wars and God has protected us and put us in a spiritual incubator. He keeps everything out of our way. He has covered us in His blood. Death had to pass over us this year and had to pass over our families. He kept us alive and in our right minds. He kept a roof over our heads. He didn't say it had to be your roof. He just kept a roof over your head. He kept you out of the rains, the floods, the hurricanes and the tornadoes. You are still here. You ought to say, "THANK YOU, JESUS, we are still here!" So you did have some news that didn't sound too good but God is still good.

REFLECT

Over the past year, how has God protected you? How has He kept you? Remember it may not be the way you wanted Him to, but He did it!

....

....

....

....

....

....

....

....

A TRIBUTE

So what? Maybe, you had something that disrupted your life and caused an inconvenience. The doctor gave you a diagnosis that sounded horrible, but God is still good because He is our source. He's not a link to our source. He is our source and we totally depend on Him. For this we are so grateful! Hallelujah! I feel like having a good old-fashioned church service today. I feel rather "churchy" today. I feel like a little Holy Ghost dance today, oh yes! I feel like going on. That's how I feel right about now. I'm giving God praise, and I hope you are too. I'm giving God glory and I hope you are too!

> *God is still good* because *He is our source.*

Stand still today and see the salvation of God. Stand still today and see what God has already pulled off on your behalf. Stand still today and watch Him demonstrate on your behalf; watch Him demonstrate His power. Let Him throw His weight around for you. Watch Him throw His glory around for you. He's waiting for you to step aside and let Him come on through your door. Somebody reading this, tell the Lord,

A TRIBUTE

- **Have Your Way, God.**
- **Have Your Way in the places we find ourselves today.**
- **Have Your Way in the earthly realm today and be glorified in us today.**
- **God be glorified in the Heavens, on the earth and be glorified in me, in us, and be pleased with our praise today.**

We are asking God to be pleased with our thanksgiving today. I feel God doing something so miraculous and so wonderful for each and every one of you, I am happy and glad about it and I celebrate you today! I celebrate the Glory of God demonstrated in your life today.

Well, my friend, He had to tell me what we were doing today. We had to give Him tribute today. He had to tell me that and I am so thankful. When He speaks to me, I hear Him and I am so thankful! He has given me the gift to hear what He has to say. And thank you for coming and seeking the Word of God. You and I have to keep hearing Him. We will not only hear Him but we will see Him. We will see Him come in great demonstration of His glory and in great demonstration of His power!

REFLECT

Give God another tribute. Where has He shown you His mercy or greatness?
Where have you seen His awesome power?

....
....
....
....
....
....
....
....
....
....
....
....
....
....
....
....
....
....
....
....

A TRIBUTE
NOTES

SWEET INSPIRATIONS

CHAPTER 9
There is Power and Purpose in Your Praise

What is the purpose of our praise? God has purpose in every praise. You have a specific impact on yourself, and everyone and everything around you when you praise. Have you ever thought about asking God, "What did my praise accomplish? Where did that praise go? What country or nation was changed for the better? What person's life was changed for the better?

Your praise has purpose and your praise has power. It has impact. As you might imagine, the Praise Reports we get on Sweet Inspirations are

> *Your praise has purpose and your praise has power.*

numerous and marvelous in their impact. We also get Praise Reports through email and our Facebook page*. What we want to do with these reports now is roll them out. We are going to be calling them out. We won't call out your name, but we will call out those praise reports coming in. We want to share them and advance them forward because that is part of the nature of praise.

> Our *praise and giving thanks* is our guarantee that *we won* before the battle even started; *before the battle began.*

Only yesterday we received some phenomenal reports but I believe we will find that the best is still to come. Our praise and giving thanks is our guarantee that we won before the battle even started; before the battle began. Think about the month ahead. This month can prove to be one of the most tremendous months of your life because God is establishing and deepening His Word in us. He has established a covenant and a promise to those who obey and follow the instruction to give Him thanks as often and as many times as they think about the goodness of God. When you do this, you will receive a total outpouring of grace and the Lord's goodness. That means just one thing— He is looking for perpetual and continual praise! That is

THERE IS POWER AND PURPOSE IN YOUR PRAISE

what we are all about, sending up a continual thanksgiving from this earthly realm into the Heart of God!

*Mother Judy Hines' contact information can be found on page 8.

REFLECT

Think about the month ahead. Write down your praises for the coming month to guarantee success before the battle even begins.

....
....
....
....
....
....
....
....
....
....
....
....
....
....
....
....

SWEET INSPIRATIONS

THERE IS POWER AND PURPOSE IN YOUR PRAISE

Earlier, we were talking about praise and we had gotten down to praising Him in good times and praising Him in bad times. We also talked about the penalty for an unwillingness to praise. Right now, let's focus on salvation and about God in control; the reasons why we praise God.

We look again to Psalm 113 verse five says, "*...there is no one else like Him.*" Verse six says, "*He knows what is going on in Heaven and on earth.*" Verse seven says, "*He raises up the poor,*" verse nine says, "*He makes the barren women have children.*" We talked about the absence of praise bringing on barrenness. We see this in countries around the world; those who fight against Christianity and those who serve other gods are in one crisis after another. You will find enormous deprivation and disease. It looks like Third World countries are just now starting to develop, because there is such a void there, an absence of praise in the earthly realm that is supposed to come up from that particular area. We say from the rising of the sun to the going down of the same. The sun rises in the east and sets in the west; and so all the places between north and south and east and west, God has commanded praises.

> God has *commanded praises.*

So, we are making the statement that we are Praise Specialists. Listen to this now. One reason we are thankful to God is for our salvation. If it were not for God, please hear this; many of us would be buried somewhere because of our poor judgment. How many reading this can testify through life you may not have always used the best judgment, and it cost you? It set you back or it caused a dilemma or a situation that took some time to get out of because you used poor judgment?

The second reason we are praising and thanking Him today is that God is in control. We should think about David. He didn't have a Bible to go by in his learning about God. First, he learned by being in fear and then by having courage. David was running from Saul. When David ran from Saul, God spared him. Do you know what it feels like to run for your life? You know you deserve justice, and then God steps in and spares you. When David sinned with Bathsheba, God forgave him. When David's own son tried to overthrow him, God rescued him.

> *God is in control.*

There is a rescue for someone reading this right now! Psalms 71:5 reads, *"For thou are my hope oh God; thou art my confidence."* Then Psalms 71:14 says, *"I will hope continually and I will praise thee yet more and more."*

THERE IS POWER AND PURPOSE IN YOUR PRAISE

REFLECT

What area of your life do you need God to rescue you from right now? Write a praise to God about His rescue from that "thing."

....
....
....
....
....
....
....
....
....
....
....
....
....

DECREE AND DECLARE

God, You are my hope and my confidence. I give you thanks and praise for rescuing me from

....
....

So, David lived the life of a man who knew God was in control. Even though he was going through troubles, David said, "I'm going to praise Him, more and more." And, folks, that is the stand you have to take even right now, today. We go through certain events, situations and circumstances; but just like David we have to say, "I'm going to praise You even yet more and more." We have to put even more and more praise on it. When trouble comes your way, the song says, "Throw your hands up and say, Hallelujah anyhow; hallelujah anyhow." You're actually saying what David said; "I know I'm in the fire; I know I'm running for my life. I know this thing doesn't look good. But I know God is in control and I'm going to praise Him yet more and more."

> I'm going to *praise God,* more and more.

That's where we are, people. We promise Him a blazing trail of thanksgiving without letting up. Sometimes we get a little weary and tired. I'm here to tell you, "Shake it off!" We are going to talk like David and we're going to say, "I'm going to even yet praise Him more and more!"

The same God, who in Genesis created the universe, who in Exodus appeared to Moses with the Ten Commandments, in I Samuel delivered David from the giant, in Job He returned to Job two-fold, in Psalms 7 offers refuge, in

THERE IS POWER AND PURPOSE IN YOUR PRAISE

Psalms 23 shows up as the Great Shepherd, in Psalms 27 is my light and my salvation, in Psalms 104 causes the grass to grow for the cattle and vegetation for man, **is the same God touching your life and reaching out to you right now.**

He is God, He is awesome, and He is in control.

So, you do not and should not have to worry about it. All you have to do is relax in The Word, flow with the Spirit of God, and obey what you hear Him say. Obey what He tells you to do. He is comfort, people. He is comfort for all of us who have lost loved ones. He is peace. For those of us who are in any type of situation; family struggles or employment struggles, He is your peace today. He is encouragement for those who are lying in the hospitals and lying in the mental institutions. He is their encouragement. For those who are facing those diagnoses, I'm here to tell you God is in control. He is strength for those of us who are even now caring for sick family members. You know sometimes when you are the caretaker, your body gets weak and tired. You can then rely on His strength and you can draw on His Strength. You can still have joy because of God's strength in your life.

SWEET INSPIRATIONS

REFLECT

Write down in one sentence what is feeling out of control in your life right now. Draw a single line through it, throw your hands up and say, "Hallelujah anyhow!"

....
....
....
....
....
....
....
....
....

Now write "Hallelujah anyhow" on the page and continue to write out a praise to God knowing He is in control.

....
....
....
....
....
....

THERE IS POWER AND PURPOSE IN YOUR PRAISE

I want to say something here on these pages, loud and clear, to put the devil in flight: **God loves you and keeps you and is soon coming back for you!** Don't forget that. So, He deserves every ounce of energy, every ounce of praise, every ounce of thanksgiving and every ounce of worship we can offer; and we can never offer Him enough. If we each had 10,000 tongues, we still could not praise Him enough. The time to praise Him is every waking moment. You don't need to find a reason; and actually you don't have to look far to give Him thanks.

> *God loves you* and keeps you and is soon *coming back for you!*

In the next few days let's accumulate some "Thanksgiving Moments." "Thanksgiving Moments" means that we know when to pipe up and say, "Thank You, Jesus. Thank You, Lord." We need to know when something happens out of our control, we need to insert a "Thank You, God. Thank You, Jesus," right there, because we are letting the world system know we are not relying on that world system, but we depend on God and His System. So, the time to praise is every waking moment. The penalty for the unwillingness to praise should never have to be our motivation because of who God is and because we have purposed in our hearts to simply give Him all the praise and all the credit.

The reason to praise is because we are here and we are blessed. Have you ever gone to the shopping mall and looked for a store and you look on the map and the map says "You are here,"? From that point, the map gives you the route to where you want to go, to your destination.

Well, THAT is what praise and thanksgiving is.

"You are here," but, if you begin to give Him, "...that yet I will praise Him; I will give Him thanksgiving yet more and more," you're going to advance mightily and see yourself progress. You will not remain the same person, nor will you remain in the same place. EVERYTHING changes. For your information, your thanksgiving and your praise is the vehicle carrying you to your next place, your next destination, your next level, and your next dimension. So, folks, we have to now beef it up!

REFLECT

Begin to accumulate "Thanksgiving Moments." Write down moments you already anticipate happening. Come back and journal your unexpected Thanksgiving Moments.

....
....
....
....
....

THERE IS POWER AND PURPOSE IN YOUR PRAISE

SWEET INSPIRATIONS

I was on my way to a meeting and I heard the Holy Ghost say these words to me; "Up your game." He was talking about a practical thing – dress code. But He said to me, "Step up your game. For where I am taking you in the future, you need to step up your game." So, when it comes to praise and when it comes to thanksgiving and when it comes to worship; we need to step it up. That means we will bring it to another level. We want to bring increase and when we bring that increase we want to experience God's Power practically, physically, and emotionally in every aspect of our lives. We'll begin to see, beyond any shadow of a doubt, the Hand of God, the Hand of Promise carrying us and bringing manifestation.

I hope you have given Him blazing thanksgiving because, well, now your wagons are loaded! I cannot wait to hear your Praise Reports!* We have gotten some so wild and fantastical you can hardly believe it. We release these Praise Reports and sometimes we just say, "Here are some from Pittsburgh, or Cleveland, or Newark, or Atlanta, and this is what happened. I want to tell you something and I want you to take it to heart right now.

God is faithful.
He is not a man that He should lie.
If He said it,
He shall surely, surely perform it.

THERE IS POWER AND PURPOSE IN YOUR PRAISE

God is faithful. He is not a man that He should lie. If He said it, He shall surely, surely perform it.

I am here to give you a Praise Report myself and that is that God is God. There is no bigger God than our God! God is God and there is no bigger God than our God. He is in control.

I am excited that God has shined on you and He has shined on me and that His glory is resting upon us; yes indeed, His glory is resting upon us. He's come to demonstrate His glory, power and ability; signs and wonders and miracles. I am excited and I want you to get excited, too. Give thanks to God for whatever He's doing on earth because wherever you are, that's where God is too. He is up to something where you are concerned. It is phenomenal, great, and it is awesome!

*Mother Judy Hines' contact information can be found on page 8.

REFLECT

How is God showing up around the world? Create Thanksgiving Moments for His glory not just in your life, but in the lives of others. Up your game. Expand your mind. Grow your relationship in God!

....

....

....

....

SWEET INSPIRATIONS

THERE IS POWER AND PURPOSE IN YOUR PRAISE

NOTES

SWEET INSPIRATIONS

CHAPTER 10
About Psalm 92...

This is only the beginning of a new lifestyle of praise and thanksgiving. A new formula. God is setting precedence in our lives. You will see what is happening when the saints stop, pause, and remember to keep God on our minds—to keep Jesus on our minds, and give Him praise and thanksgiving continually throughout the day. It is phenomenal!

Let's consider Psalm 92. I want to read it from multiple translations. Psalm 92 is a song for the Sabbath Day and says,

> *It is a good and delightful thing to give thanks to the Lord, to sing praises [with musical accompaniment] to Your name, O Most High, To show forth Your loving-kindness in the morning, and Your faithfulness by night...* (AMPC)

That means when you give God praise and thanksgiving,

you are a witness of His loving kindness early in the morning and His faithfulness by night. In the morning, His loves wakes us up. In the evening, His faithfulness keeps us out of harm's way and allows us to get a good night's rest; allows us to lay down in peace; allows us to be protected during the night and gives us our blanket of security around the world; which is better than anything the military could ever give us. His faithfulness gives us what guns and weapons cannot do for us. All of this and more is what God does for us.

> His *faithfulness* gives us what *guns and weapons cannot* do for us.

In the Common English Bible it says,

> *It is good to give thanks to the LORD, to sing praises to your name, Most High; to proclaim your loyal love in the morning, your faithfulness at nighttime with the ten-stringed harp, with the melody of the lyre because you've made me happy...*

ABOUT PSALM 92...

And in the Message Bible it says,

What a beautiful thing, God, to give thanks, to sing an anthem to you, the High God! To announce your love each daybreak, sing your faithful presence all through the night, Accompanied by dulcimer and harp, the full-bodied music of strings. You made me so happy, God

I'm telling you, we always have many, many things to praise God for! It's show and tell time, people, in the Kingdom of God. We are completing an assignment. We have been obedient to what God told us to do and He's going to bless, anoint, and break through to us because of our level of obedience to give Him in our days of thanksgiving; as we give Him continual thanksgiving coming up from the earthly realm straight into His Heart. It has been a sweet aroma in the nostrils of God, because we have faith; we have believed God, and taken Him at His Word.

Now we shall see the great things God has on His mind concerning us before the foundation of the world! We have met the requirements and God is going to show you what happens when you meet His requirements; meet His

> We always have *many, many things to praise* God for!

commands; fulfill His wish and His vision. God has had great delight in His people praising him because He has found a people who will not only obey but a people who know that we owe Him thanksgiving and praise! Hallelujah!

REFLECT

What blessings are you seeing already from your praise? What do you desire from God? Remember His promises to you – and continue to give Him praise!

....
....
....
....
....
....
....
....
....
....
....
....
....
....
....

ABOUT PSALM 92...

Earlier, when I was reading about the word "tribute," the writer said we owe God "rent." I had to back up, and then I remembered we are just passing through this place. This is not our home. This is not our resting place. Eternal life is not here on Earth. This physical existence is temporary. So, He has allowed us to be here in this earthly realm for a certain amount of time; but this, folks, is not it. We are almost like squatters or share-croppers, but even those words are not quite the right ones. We are working the land like they worked the land back in the old days. They knew that although they were going through great trials, hardships, and torture that their reward was not here on Earth. We got most of our songs and hymns from the slaves who were under such tremendous pressure and strain.

> Although they were *going through great trials, hardships, and torture,* their reward was not here on Earth.

But can you imagine the miracle that they still had joy, happiness, and peace? They were still able to praise God and give Him thanksgiving! They were still able to sing about His love and His greatness while they were still going through it all. They could still sing His praises while in the midst of pain, suffering, and while they were experiencing the death of their beloveds all around them.

I'm telling you, today we have something to praise God for and to give Him thanks for, because He allows us to walk in the newness of life. He allows us to freely praise Him; He allows us to pick and choose vocations. I'm telling you these little things we take for granted, we should not EVER take for granted. The reason we can experience these great things is because of His loyalty; His loving loyalty toward us and His loving kindness toward us. It is amazing; and here in America, we take so much for granted that other countries cannot experience!

- **They have to go underground to read the Bible!**
- **They are persecuted for reading the Bible!**
- **Some modern-day saints have been decapitated for reading the Bible!**
- **Some have been martyred in this modern day; as we sleep.**

Here in America, while we sleep, we have no idea who is going through persecution because of their love for God—because they take a brave stand for God.

About Psalm 92...

REFLECT

Take a moment to research some modern day Christian martyrs. Visit The Voice of the Martyrs website. Pray and give God praise for what He is doing around the world.

We drove into a beautiful town in the Southeast the other night, and my niece needed to stop at a store. We found one and went inside where we found the owners—a husband and wife team. The wife and husband are Christians who decided they didn't want their shop to operate under the yoke of organized crime anymore.

They loved God.

They decided they would no longer allow themselves to be bullied. They went to the local "bosses" and told them they were no longer going to be under the rule and control of the crime organization. These souls love God and want to serve Him and Him only.

So, these criminals beat the couple so badly they were unrecognizable. The husband told us how he couldn't even recognize his wife because they had beaten and disfigured her, and how he had also been beaten so viciously. Then, he told us how much he loves God and the only reason he could go through that violence and absorb that violence was because of his great love for God.

> In spite of everything, *God is still a good God.*

I don't know how many of us could say the same thing, but God knows what we can endure.

It was amazing to us to hear the testimony of this young

ABOUT PSALM 92...

man, still giving God thanks and still giving God the glory after that unbelievably horrible nightmare he and his wife lived through! However, God has prospered their way.

I want to tell you right now that in spite of everything, God is still a good God. Even with tears streaming down our face, our hands thrown up in despair, and having the feeling that we don't know where His salvation will come from, from one day to the next; God is still good. He still reigns supreme, and we owe Him praise and thanksgiving.

REFLECT

Ask God to increase your faith in His faithfulness that you will be prepared and able to do whatever He asks of you. What is God asking of you right now?

....
....
....
....
....
....
....
....
....
....

SWEET INSPIRATIONS

ABOUT PSALM 92...

*L*et's take a look at the closing of this devotional, now. Hallelujah! Hallelujah! The last couple of verses of this scripture read,

The righteous will spring up like a palm tree. They will grow strong like a cedar of Lebanon. Those who have been replanted in the LORD's house will spring up in the courtyards of our God. They will bear fruit even when old and gray; they will remain lush and fresh in order to proclaim: The LORD is righteous. He's my rock. There's nothing unrighteous in Him.

Hallelujah! Hallelujah! Let's look at Verse 11. It says,

My eyes have seen my enemies' defeat; my ears have heard the downfall of my evil foes.

I want you to know you will see some things in your own life you didn't think you would see; things that haven't even crossed your mind. You haven't imagined what great things our great God will perform on your behalf. Continue in that frame of praise, that frame of mind and soul where you expect a miracle; continue in worship and thanksgiving.

> *Continue in that frame of praise*, that frame of mind and soul where *you expect a miracle.*

As I always say, "Go to the mode of celebration and stay there!" Your "celebration mode" gives God greater access to the earthly realm. It gives Him power to do even more because we become part of the group called, "He That Believeth."

We believe and take Him at His Word.

Remember, Jesus couldn't do much in Nazareth because they did not believe, but I'm here to tell you the group reading these pages right now believes God. We do take Him at His Word. Whatever He says, it is so, and so it is. We stand in the midst of nothing less than the supernatural, and the miraculous, and the supernatural and the miraculous is what we have embarked upon. He has promised and He is the Promise-keeper. He has made covenant with us and He is the Covenant- keeper. So, get ready, get ready, get ready! That's what Bishop T. D. Jakes always says. But we are on "Ready" right now, so we are partial to receive what God has spoken. We are tuned in to God's frequency, so to speak, and there is not one thing the enemy can do about it.

> Go to the *mode of celebration* and *stay there!*

ABOUT PSALM 92...

REFLECT

Over the course of this devotional we have increased our thanksgiving, praise and worship.

Now let's increase our level of belief and expectation of God's supernatural power. Decree and declare what you are believing God for!

I'm excited about what God is up to where you are concerned. I'm excited about what God is pulling off on your behalf and I'm excited about God bringing blessings to you, through you, and for you. I'm excited about this impact we are having right now, worldwide, because a few of us have chosen to do the will of God. This has been a great period of thanksgiving and the best is still yet to come! Eyes have not seen and ears have not heard, nor has it entered into our minds what God is on the verge of doing on behalf of you, and you, and you. So, get ready folks. Don't let the enemy bring those thoughts of defeat; don't let the enemy make you feel less than perfect or even inadequate. Don't let the enemy tell you, "Nothing is happening…"

> *Do not allow anything* to penetrate your spirit and *get you off your game.*

I want you to get up, get indignant in the Holy Ghost, and look the enemy straight in the eye and tell him, "My God is bigger! My God is bigger than you and my God is bigger than any other god! He shall do exactly what He said He is going to do!" God is stepping up to the plate, folks, and unlike that baseball player they called "The Babe," God does not even have to point in the direction where He is hitting the ball on our behalf! We know where He is hitting

ABOUT PSALM 92...

it for us, and it is not into the stands. It's not even out of the park. It is right out of this world!

The Lord Himself needs you to "up your game" and put on a happy face today. I want you to get up from wherever you are right now. I want you to shake off everything that is not like God; don't allow that parasite to attach itself to you. Do not allow anything to penetrate your spirit and get you off your game. Now is the time for us to move out, folks. We need to sail out of the shallow waters in the harbor and move out to the deep water. See your salvation in The Hand of God and move like you have never moved before. That is why we are here. That is what we are here for, and we shall see it. Oh yeah, we shall see it! Hallelujah!

REFLECT

"Go to the mode of celebration and stay there!" Describe in as much detail as possible your mode(s) of celebration in the Lord and what you do to stay there.

....
....
....
....
....
....
....
....

SWEET INSPIRATIONS

ABOUT PSALM 92...
NOTES

SWEET INSPIRATIONS

CHAPTER 11
Revive!

Today, we look to the word "revive," and in Psalm 119:88 we find it reads,

> *"Revive me according to Your Loving Kindness."*

Now, when I think about the word "revive," I think of phrases like, "a breath of fresh air," "something new," or "a fresh start." God answered David's prayer and did revive him and that revival of Spirit was all according to God's loving kindness.

What God needs us to see right here is that God did exactly what was requested. What we need to do throughout the day is thank God for His faithfulness in answering us every day in every way. He fulfills our needs. If you are having what seems to you to be a rough day, remember, we can depend on God. We can depend on Him alone

> He is our *God of all comfort*

and He is the One who will see us through no matter what. He is our God of hope; He is our God of all comfort (II Corinthians 1:3). He is ever faithful to His promises and He is our salvation. That's what we want to think about today. We need to think and pray about it. He gives us the reviving power we need to rise above any and all of our negative circumstances and to continue to rise in His presence and His glory. God gives us the reviving power we need to rise above our present circumstances and to continue to move forward in His Light—His Love.

Think about this. The enemy likes to take holidays, weekends, vacations, time off, or any other usually happy, restful time for us and wreak absolute havoc in the lives of both believers and non-believers. For most of us, we really do look forward to these times as opportunities to revive a lot of things. We catch up on rest, we revive our friendships and family relationships, and look forward to hobbies or activities that truly give us that spiritual sustenance that increases our personal happiness and allow us to give more glory to the Lord. That is right when the enemy steps in. The enemy needs to take us to a kind of "mental landscape" where our happiness and joy can easily become afflicted and tormented. Somebody loses hope. Someone faints on the sidewalk. Somebody throws in the towel on a relationship. Someone gives in to the lies and the afflictions of the enemy. Happiness, joy, and opportunities for revival of all sorts just seem to up and leave the scene. When people suffer this hopelessness, they sometimes even go so far as to try to take their own lives.

Read this note again and again: God gives us the reviving power we need to rise above our circumstances and continue onward.

> God gives us the *reviving power* we need to *rise above our circumstances and continue onward.*

Children, whatever you do, do NOT "throw in the towel" on YOUR Dreams, YOUR Visions, YOUR Missions, and YOUR Assignments God has given to YOU.

He shall, and He will, revive you.

Again, this is our anchor phrase today and it is from Psalms 119:88 reading, "Revive me according to your loving kindness."

SWEET INSPIRATIONS

REFLECT

What areas of your life do you need a Holy Ghost revival? Ask God to give you the power and hope to rise above your circumstances.

REVIVE!

We need to once again speak, think, and act out of the word "hope." Too many people have lost hope and they've lost faith. Hope-faith; faith-hope. Your hope lies not within you or your circumstances. You have to, you must, look to the Lord. Obey His Word. Then, when you do look to the Lord and obey His Word, you can look ahead. You can look beyond present circumstances. You can look up around the corner with confidence, because you have a future. God's promises are sure and His Word is true.

Your hope in God should motivate you into giving thanks to Him. He loves you. The believer stands between blessings received and blessings hoped for. Therefore, we should always be giving thanks. We should remain in that "thankful mode." His blessings are continuous and everlasting. In the moment before you can even turn around to thank Him, another blessing comes right in! Your hope in God and in His Word revives and increases your steadfastness. Your hope increases the steadfastness of the Holy Ghost in you. God moves you up a level and our hope provides us with our solid foundation. I Thessalonians

> The believer stands between *blessings received* and *blessings hoped for.*

1:3 reads,

> *We give thanks to God always, for all of you, making mention of you in our prayers, constantly bearing in mind your work of faith and labor of love, and steadfastness of hope in the Lord Jesus Christ in the presence of our God and Father.*

The root source of the Thessalonians' hope is the Lord Jesus Christ, firmly built on nothing less than Jesus' blood and righteousness. Therefore, OUR faith WE must build on nothing less than Jesus' blood and His righteousness. The fruit of that faith is our steadfastness and endurance in Him. I always say this:

"When I was going through the aneurysm, and two strokes, I was not a survivor. A survivor is by chance. I endure."

You endure by choice. I chose to endure the pain of healing. I had two choices.

I could choose the pain of not healing or I could choose the pain of healing. I chose to endure the pain of healing.

So, you have to be steadfast.

This steadfastness becomes a spirit-empowered quality in a you giving you the ability to bear up triumphantly!

REVIVE!

REFLECT

Are you ready to choose steadfastness and hope? Set your mind on God's goodness and faithfullness. Write out statments confirming your decision now.

Now here is another phrase we will talk about more in the future, but take this into your heart right now—Dokimazo (Dok-im-ad'-zo) Power. Dokimazo is a verb that comes to us from Ancient Greek meaning "to bear up triumphantly in the face of much tribulation and suffering." In other words, when something difficult and disappointing happens in your life, and you make the choice to endure it, to bear up triumphantly in its face, you become enabled by the Spirit of Grace to look upon the natural and supernatural worlds with the eyes of faith! And when you look with the eyes of faith to Christ and His power and His All-sufficiency, and you refuse to give in to complaining or bitterness, then **your faith perseveres.** Then, you are deploying your **Dokimazo Power.**

> Dokimazo: a verb meaning *"to bear up triumphantly* in the *face of much tribulation and suffering."*

I want to say that again: *If something happens in your life that is difficult and disappointing and you make the choice to endure it, to bear up triumphantly in its face, you are going to be enabled and empowered by the Spirit of Grace to look with the eyes of faith; not with natural sight; you're going to look to Christ and to His Power and His All-sufficiency and you are going to refuse to give in to complaining or bitterness. That is when your faith perseveres. HALLELUJAH!*

In the Book of Thessalonians, these same folks in the Lord Jesus Christ, brought forth this fragrant fruit of steadfastness, which, in turn, enabled them to bear up under their many trials and tribulations. Dokimazo says your trials and your tribulations are your classroom. Furthermore, when we live with an expectant hope, our lifestyle will give clear evidence of the genuineness, the authenticity, the reality of salvation in our lives. And when our lives give testimony to that salvation, you most definitely have something fantastic to celebrate and you celebrate with the giving of thanks.

We are talking about hope, tribulation, persevering, and proven character. Hope, which does not disappoint, because the Love of God has been poured out in our hearts through the Holy Spirit Who has given everything to us. Sometimes, hope is waiting, among other things. Expected waiting was a lifestyle in the earlier days of the church. Expected waiting is something we can still use more of in today's world, as well.

> Dokimazo says your *trials and your tribulations* are *your classroom.*

SWEET INSPIRATIONS

REFLECT

When have you experienced Dokimazo Power? How did it feel? What were the miracles from God. Put a praise on it and ask God for more!

REVIVE!

We celebrate every day because God has seen fit to honor us for our ministry. I love and appreciate you all. Remember that today you are getting a breath of fresh air. God is going to breathe new life into you and He is going to revive you. Revive, according to Psalm 119:88 is

"...a breath of fresh air, heavenly air and He is reviving."

Remember to give Him thanks and be steadfast with your thankfulness today.

God is faithful.

If you are having a rough day, remember, you can depend on Him. Old Zion says, "...you can depend on God." Remember, you can depend on Him. He is your God, your hope, your comfort, and He is ever faithful to His Promises. So, submit to the Lord and trust in Him. He is going to give you the reviving power you need to rise above your circumstances and continue forward in His Light—His Love.

Have a wonderful, wonderful Jesus-filled day. God bless.

SWEET INSPIRATIONS

REFLECT

Copy this in your own handwriting: God will give me the reviving power I need to rise above my circumstances and continue.

REVIVE!

NOTES

SWEET INSPIRATIONS

CHAPTER 12
Just Begin...

This morning when I woke up, early as usual, a beginning thought came to me and of course, the thought came from God. I know it was from God. He said, "Tell the people of God that if the disciples had never begun, if they had never started to speak, there would be no Pentecost." There would be no power of the Holy Ghost as we experience it and know it today. So what He wants you to know is that when you hit that "unfamiliar" area, when you hit that "uncomfortable" zone, when you find yourself outside of your comfort zone, when you hit that zone that says, "I don't know," you're going

> God is *orchestrating* something *bigger* than you and *bigger* than me.

to still have to take a step of faith and believe God and know He is orchestrating something bigger than you and bigger than me. All you have to do is just begin. I want you to write that down this morning. Just begin, because God wants and needs you to understand something. You have now embarked upon something truly great, and a new beginning, as if we were starting this entire New Year all over again. He's telling you that this moment right now is absolutely the newest of a new beginning.

There was a storm that arose out over the ocean. And that storm thought that it was going to conquer those who were at sea. Then we heard the Spirit of God say, "Peace. Peace. Be still." That was something the storm probably had never heard before. But it had to obey.

What is Mother Judy saying to you? God is likely asking you to do some things you have never done before. But the power of God has everything under His command and has already commanded the resources and the provision to obey and find you for this new beginning. He has composed, arranged, and orchestrated it for your life. He says, "All YOU need to do is begin!" God reminds us if the disciples had never started speaking, then other people in other nations would have never heard the Good News preached in their native tongue. So, even though it seems to you like something is impossible, overwhelming, it seems there's nobody else doing it and it seems like there's nobody else coming along; remember—it just seems like that.

JUST BEGIN...

REFLECT

You have been thinking of something lately that now needs a beginning. God Himself needs you to "Just begin." What is it?

The majority is already on your side. God represents the majority! He represents the majority, so you don't have to worry about whether or not you're going to make it. You don't have to worry about whether or not you're going to be successful. He has already ordained it so, and He has already written your success story. I want you to get up, and say today and every day,

> ***I'm having a brand new beginning.***
> ***Every day I'm going to start. Every day***
> ***I'm going to begin. Every day I'm going to***
> ***take a new step.***

So right now, shake off that state of stupor, that state of despair, and that state of negativity that has attached itself to your life like a parasite. Listen my friends, you are ready to go out there today and turn this old world upside down! Shake it up! Turn this world upside down and let this earthly realm know God has someone on the wall willing and obedient and who WILL take that first step and just begin.

There are some entrepreneurs reading this and He's telling you, "Just start!" You've been playing with your idea. You've been thinking about it. You've been trying to put things in place but today, right now, the Holy Spirit says, "YOU WILL make great strides." Yes, you are going to make great strides because God is about to send the winds of strength

JUST BEGIN...

and provision right at your back. There are readers on this page right now who absolutely, positively need a brand-new start. You have encountered some things that have wearied you and made you become, not lackadaisical, but you have been dragging your feet a little bit. You're shuffling from side to side and the Holy Spirit says, "It's time to move! It's time to arrive now! It's time to conquer! It's time to go over that wall!" I'll tell you one thing my friend, the enemy cannot stop you. He cannot deter you, and he cannot cause you to miss this moment. Only you can do that. Only you can cause yourself to miss your moment.

> God is about to send the *winds of strength* and *provision right at your back.*

REFLECT

What five things are you going to do to move your vision forward? Praise God and take that leap!

....
....
....
....
....
....

Sweet Inspirations

JUST BEGIN...

I am excited this morning because there's going to be a major thrust in the earth. Your churches are about to be filled to the utmost. Your churches are going to go to overflow capacity as far as membership is concerned. I hear the Lord say, "There is a new birthing on Earth." I heard Earth when it gulped. I heard Earth had to yield up the increase. Some of you have been toiling very, very hard lately. You've been toiling and not seeing the benefits or the fruits of your labor. But the Holy Ghost has turned toward us today with great intensity. Mark it. Put a date beside it or write it on your calendar. He turns away from other things, looks precisely in our direction and pronounces that "Some phenomenal things are about to surface as far as you, you, and you are concerned!"

> *The Holy Ghost* has turns toward us today *with great intensity.*

Get ready. There's an entire phenomenon that's about to push forward and He's going to use some of you who are even reading this right now. I see people approaching you—other pastors who are not doing well, but they are going to come alongside you and find out that YOU are a source of strength for them. They are going to find out you are a person with a network. They are going to find out you can provide technical assistance and support. They're going to find out you are full of the wisdom of God. I hear the Lord say, "Welcome, my children! Step into your new day because this is it."

Isn't that amazing? That's the word we started with earlier and here it is again. God says He's turning in your direction! The same way the snow melts every year, God is about to pour out His anointing on you. A fresh and new anointing is coming your way. I hear the Lord say the wind is going to cause the trees to sway and they're going to be swaying from side to side and that's what you are going to be doing under this anointing. You're going to be swaying under that power and that wind is going to push you into that prophetic moment that you've been taught about, reading about, and studying about here!

He says, "Welcome to that prophetic moment."

Oh yes, God is up to something where His people are concerned. There is absolutely going to be an explosion now! You know what? I've been undergoing such tremendous warfare and I am telling God, "Thank you for the warfare! It has increased my anointing and made my gift even keener, more sensitive. I sense the Holy Spirit flowing like never before!"

> God says He's *turning in your direction!*

JUST BEGIN...

So everybody reading this right now, get ready to lift those hands and give God glory. Listen, nobody can hear you. You can have a "Hallelujah good time," because this is it. This is your morning, your moment, your time. God is absolutely going to pull it all together for you. There will be no let up now that the floodgates have opened. I can hear the Lord saying, "Full speed ahead!" I hear Him say, "Quantum leap!" I hear Him say, "The winds of adversity have already been commanded to blow in your favor." So, this morning I want you to get ready because this is a most exciting time to be alive in the Kingdom. You are really living in your finest hour. You are now beginning to have a most refining moment. God is about to do His greatest work for you and do His greatest work through you. Oh my goodness! I feel the wind pushing me! I feel the breath of God pushing me! I'm speaking to some churches and children in the Midwest, now. The Holy Spirit says, "You have experienced a dry season, but now, that has lifted. It has lifted, and there is going to be an onslaught of growth that's coming into your churches, coming into your individual ministries, and all He needs for you to do is to remember His Word. Say it is so, and so it is."

SWEET INSPIRATIONS

REFLECT

What is God saying to you? What are the next steps He wants you to take to experience this move of God?

....
....
....
....
....
....
....
....
....
....
....
....
....
....
....
....
....
....
....
....

JUST BEGIN...

There's going to be a report of a miracle that's going to be so phenomenal we will hear about it on CNN and on all the major networks because God is about to show you how He can touch the king's heart and make the king bless his servants and bless His people. I'm telling you, get ready. This is better than having the sweepstakes people show up with a million-dollar check at your front door! This is something far greater. God has something more phenomenal that's going to make the world turn its eye and see how great He takes care of His people!

Get ready, because there's a cloud of glory headed your way! I hear the Lord saying in the next thirty days there's going to be the shift where YOU need to accomplish His will like never before. So, we need to be excited on these pages today. We need to be so excited and telling God, "Thank you!" We need to tell Him He's the only true God. He is, and without God we are nothing. I want you all to know that today is it! We are born today!

Well, my friend, that's about all we have for *Sweet Inspirations, Volume II*. As you can imagine I'm on my way to my next engagement, maybe near you. I certainly hope so. But wherever Mother is in the physical sense I am by your side in the spiritual sense and remember this: we are **Prayer Warriors** together. Side by side, we can anticipate the greatest move of God ever! I know that He will not cause us to be denied or disappointed. I believe this is the day God takes all of us off that street called "Delay," and puts us on "Acceleration," for what He has promised. He brings us into the Promised Land. He brings us the increase of the land and causes the land to yield up the increase we have been waiting on.

All right! God bless you! We just thank God! We just want everybody to know that when you close the last pages of **The Morning Cup: A Sweet Inspirations Collection Volume II**, that your brand-new day has only begun! God is going to just literally blow your mind today! I tell you, I am just so empowered, and I believe that everybody reading these lines right now is going to go out into your life empowered today by the power of God! The glory of God in all of us has already begun! Bless you! Bless you! Bless you—and you too! We will see you soon, and talk in the morning! God Bless.

JUST BEGIN...
NOTES

SWEET INSPIRATIONS

ABOUT THE AUTHOR

Judy L. Hines, a native North Carolinian presently residing in the State of Georgia, has served the Body of Christ in major capacities for over 40 years. She is a dynamic Preacher of the Gospel, a Pastors' Pastor, and author. A frequent keynote speaker for national audiences, Mother Hines', approach to the Gospel and the mandate to build Kingdom, is revolutionary and effective!

Mother Hines is Founder and Overseer of Overcomer International Network (overcomerintlnet.org) and The School of the Spirit, and served as Pastor of School of the Spirit Fellowship Church. Since 1994, she has traveled extensively in a full-time prophetic, teaching and deliverance ministry, establishing and overseeing churches and affiliate ministries, worldwide.

As an international spokesperson, she has seen thousands of lives changed, set free and delivered. Mother Hines operates in the gifts of the spirit and flows under a Powerful Prophetic Anointing. Her ministry is followed by awesome demonstrations of God's power through the Holy Spirit transcending the barriers of denomination, race, culture and gender.

You are an overcomer, so get connected to the Overcomer International Network!

Be one of the first to know about the upcoming teachings, classes, conferences, and events of Mother Judy Hines and her Eagle's Gathering team. Visit the website, www.overcomerintlnet.org or connect with Mother on Facebook.

 @OvercomerIntlNet

 @SweetInspirationsWithMotherJudyHines

The Morning Cup

A SWEET INSPIRATIONS COLLECTION ~ VOL 1
by Mother Judy Hines

Do you want to step into the life that Jesus died for you to have? Let me ask, what is in your morning cup? Mother Judy Hines has blessed many people over the last 9 years to start their day off right through her Sweet Inspiration call. She is excited to help you fill your morning cup by illuminating the Bible and the promises of God through these life changing morning devotionals. As you dive into this book you will experience the very presence of the Father. He shall give you the very sentiments of His heart. You will become His penmanship in the earth realm. This book is filled with thoughts that will not only inspire you, but lift you to new levels, dimension and horizons.

ISBN-13: 978-1732287907   ©2018

talking *to* GOD

by Mother Judy Hines

Throughout all of life today, a certain sound consumes us. When you quiet yourself and become still you hear it pierce the air. The sound that rings out is an all-points bulletin for prayers. Prayers are A.W.O.L. Prayers are missing in action. When prayers become missing in action, the enemy comes not to play, but to steal, maim, destroy and kill. The enemy has destroyed many souls and taken many more captive by sad situations and mundane scenarios of daily life. We must now "have a little talk with God." Let us bring our prisoners of war, the absent without leave, and the missing in action home. Let us help heal them, set them free, deliver them from evil, and make them whole once more. God needs us to get out in the battlefield. He needs our most effective fervent prayers.

ISBN-13: 978-1628395617 ©2013

www.ingramcontent.com/pod-product-compliance
Lightning Source LLC
Chambersburg PA
CBHW052020070526
44584CB00016B/1837